Family Circle | dessert cookbook

Family Circle.

DESSERT
COOKBOOK

FAMILY CIRCLE LIBRARY OF CREATIVE COOKING

A Practical Guide to creative cooking containing special material from Family Circle Magazine and the Family Circle Illustrated Library of Cooking

ROCKVILLE HOUSE PUBLISHERS
GARDEN CITY, NEW YORK 11530

on the cover:
Fruit desserts in all their glory are here in this attractive display: **Frozen Papaya Cream** (bottom), **Summer Pudding Surprise** (right) **Lemon Meringue Tarts, Minted Pineapple Cake** (left) and a bowl of ripe fruits.

on the back cover:
As varied as they come, **Strawberry Mousse** (bottom) and chess pies (top) are sure to please any dessert-lover.

opposite title page:
When you are looking for that extra-special dessert, try **Spanische Windtorte**—a meringue with a surprise filling.

Publishing Staff

Editor: MALCOLM E. ROBINSON
Design and Layout: MARGOT L. WOLF
Production Editor: DONALD D. WOLF

For Family Circle

Editorial Director: ARTHUR M. HETTICH
Editor Family Circle Books: MARIE T. WALSH
Assistant Editor: CERI E. HADDA

A QUICK METRIC TABLE FOR COOKS

Liquid Measures

1 liter	4¼ cups (1 quart + ¼ cup or 34 fluid ounces)	1 gallon	3.785 liters
1 demiliter (½ liter)	2⅛ cups (1 pint + ⅛ cups or 17 fluid ounces)	1 quart	0.946 liter
1 deciliter (1/10 liter)	A scant ½ cup or 3.4 fluid ounces	1 pint	0.473 liter
1 centiliter (1/100 liter)	Approximately 2 teaspoons or .34 fluid ounce	1 cup	0.237 liter or 237 milliliters
1 milliliter (1/1000 liter)	Approximately 1/5 teaspoon or .034 fluid ounce	1 tbsp.	Approximately 1.5 centiliters or 15 milliliters

Weights

1 kilogram	2.205 pounds	1 pound	0.454 kilogram or 453.6 grams
500 grams	1.103 pounds or about 17.5 ounces	½ pound	0.226 kilogram or 226.8 grams
100 grams	3.5 ounces	¼ pound	0.113 kilogram or 113.4 grams
10 grams	.35 ounce	1 ounce	28.35 grams
1 gram	0.035 ounce		

Linear Measures

1 meter	1.09 yards or 3.28 feet or 39.37 inches	1 yard	0.914 meter
1 decimeter (1/10 meter)	3.93 inches	1 foot	0.3048 meter or 3.048 decimeters or 30.48 centimeters
1 centimeter (1/100 meter)	0.39 inch	1 inch	2.54 centimeters or 25.4 millimeters
1 millimeter (1/1000 meter)	0.039 inch		

Contents

INTRODUCTION 6

1. EYE-DAZZLING FRUIT DESSERTS 7

2. FROZEN DESSERT SENSATIONS 25

3. REFRIGERATED DESSERT SPLENDORS 41
    Tortes 41
    Cheesecakes 47
    Bavarians 49
    Gelatins 52

4. EXCITING PASTRIES AND PIES 57
    Shortcakes 57
    Chess Pies 59
    Meringues 65

5. MEMORABLE PUDDINGS 69
    Custards 69
    Souffles 73
    Cremes 77
    Puddings 80

6. SAUCES AND TOPPINGS 87

INDEX 95

Fruit desserts in all their glory are here in this attractive display: **Frozen Papaya Cream** (bottom), **Summer Pudding Surprise** (right) **Lemon Meringue Tarts, Minted Pineapple Cake** (left) and a bowl of ripe fruits.

Introduction

YOU WANT A DESSERT, but you're not sure which one. This is a common problem for the cook. Everybody has a dessert favorite. Unfortunately, this all too often means that someone is disappointed. You can take away this problem with one of the many new dessert recipes in this book.

And for your ease in finding the right surprise, the recipes are grouped so you can find them without having to page through the book (although this is pleasant). But, this is done with your interests at heart.

Check through EYE-DAZZLING FRUIT DESSERTS, then leaf through REFRIGERATED DESSERT SPLENDORS. Just these two sections will give you more ideas than you can deal with in a month of Sundays.

And there are six individual sections like these. Where possible, each has been divided so that you can find a cheesecake or a souffle, or a custard, or a shortcake that you like. In fact, there are so many variations of familiar favorites, that no one need be upset with your choice. The chocolate lover and the parfait fan will rejoice at the chocolate parfait. And this type of cross-over has been done throughout the book.

So, enjoy your **Dessert Cookbook,** created with you in mind and with your dessert-interests at heart.

Eye-Dazzling Fruit Desserts

There's more to a fruit dessert than some fruit, maybe some gelatin, and the refrigerator, as you'll learn when you page through this chapter. The recipes and illustrations show you many rich and varied ways of presenting all-season fruits in desserts that everyone will want again.

Minted Pineapple Cake

Easy-to-make chiffon cake soaked in a light pineapple-and-mint syrup, then filled with fresh pineapple and strawberries just before serving

Makes 10 to 12 servings.

PINEAPPLE CHIFFON CAKE
(see index for recipe)
1¾ cups unsweetened pineapple juice
¾ cup sugar
½ cup coarsely chopped fresh mint
   OR: 2 tablespoons dried mint
1 medium-size ripe pineapple
1 pint strawberries
   Sprigs of mint
   Green grapes

1 Prepare cake; cool. Place cake on serving plate.
2 Combine pineapple juice and sugar in medium-size saucepan; bring to boiling, stirring often, until sugar is dissolved; boil, uncovered, 5 minutes. Remove from heat; stir in mint and let stand 5 to 10 minutes for mint flavor to develop. (Taste occasionally until flavor is as strong as you like it.) Strain syrup into a small bowl. Measure out ½ cup; reserve.
3 Gradually brush remaining warm syrup over cake until all is absorbed. (This can be done the day before.) Refrigerate.
4 Pare, quarter and core pineapple; cut each quarter crosswise into thin slices. Place slices in large bowl; add ⅔ of reserved syrup. Hull strawberries and cut in half; place in medium-size bowl; add remaining syrup. Let both fruits stand to macerate 30 minutes.
5 Just before serving, fill center of cake with fruits; serve any extra fruit mixture and juice in a separate bowl.
6 Garnish with sprigs of mint and small bunches of green grapes. Serve with softly whippped cream, if you wish.

Lemon Meringue Tarts

Both the crisp meringues and the velvety lemon custard filling are nice to have on hand: at dessert time just fill as many meringues as needed and top with fresh berries or sliced fruit

Bake at 250° for 30 minutes.
Makes 12 servings.

MERINGUES
3 egg whites
⅛ teaspoon cream of tartar
¾ cup sugar

LEMON CUSTARD FILLING
3 egg yolks
1 whole egg
¾ cup sugar
2 tablespoons grated lemon rind
⅓ cup lemon juice
½ cup (1 stick) butter or margarine
   Assorted fruits

1 Line one large or two small cookie sheets with brown paper. Outline 12 ovals, about 4x2-inches, on paper.
2 Make meringues: beat egg whites with cream of tartar in a large bowl until foamy and double in volume. Sprinkle in sugar, 1 tablespoon at a time, beating constantly with mixer at high speed until sugar is dissolved completely and meringue stands in firm peaks when beater is lifted slowly. (Beating will take 10 to 15 minutes.)
3 Spoon meringue into pastry bag fitted with a star tip. Pipe into outlines on paper, building up sides slightly to form a shell, or spoon meringue into outline, building up sides with tip of spoon.
4 Bake in a very slow oven (250°) 30 minutes. Turn off heat and leave meringues in oven with door closed at least 1 hour or overnight. When cool, store in container with tight-fitting cover. (They will keep several weeks.)
5 Make LEMON CUSTARD FILLING: Combine egg yolks, egg and sugar in top of double boiler; mix well. Stir in lemon rind, lemon juice and butter. Cook over simmering water, stirring constantly, 10 to 15 minutes, or until mixture thickens. Remove from heat; cool. Spoon into jars; cover tightly. (Can be stored in refrigerator several days, or stored in freezer for weeks.)

(continued)

6 When ready to fill shells, spoon about 2 tablespoons filling into each meringue shell. Top with fresh berries or sliced fruits of your choice.

Summer Pudding Surprise

This traditional English dessert does not require any cooking: the juices of the fresh sugared berries spooned inside the bread-lined mold soak into the bread when refrigerated overnight

Makes 8 servings.

3 cups fresh sliced strawberries
1 pint fresh or frozen unsweetened blueberries
⅓ to ½ cup sugar
1 package (10 ounces) frozen raspberries,
  partially thawed
10 slices firm white bread
1 cup heavy cream

1 Place strawberries and blueberries in large bowl; stir in sugar. Let stand, stirring often, until juicy and sugar is dissolved, about 30 minutes. Stir in raspberries.
2 Meanwhile, remove crusts from bread slices. Line a 1½-quart deep mixing bowl with 6 or 7 overlapping bread slices. Cut one slice to fit bottom. Fill bowl with berry mixture; cover top completely with remaining bread. Cover with wax paper; set a small flat plate or pie plate on top and place a 3- to 4-pound weight on the plate. (Several large cans of fruit or vegetables will do.) The weighted plate presses on the bread to compact the mixture. Refrigerate overnight.
3 To serve, invert pudding onto a chilled serving plate. Garnish with a few extra berries, if you wish. Cut pudding in wedges to serve. Beat the cream just until softly whipped. Serve with the pudding.

Frozen Papaya Cream

This unusual and delicious dessert is made from the tropical papaya fruit, a relative newcomer to the supermarket

Makes 4 servings.

2 papayas
4 tablespoons lime juice
⅓ cup sugar
½ cup heavy cream
  Lime wedges

1 Cut papayas in half lengthwise; scoop out and discard seeds. Scoop out 4 small balls with a melon baller, reserving for garnish. Carefully scoop out remaining pulp, reserving papaya shells. Puree papaya with lime juice and sugar in container of electric blender until smooth or beat with a fork or rotary beater until fairly smooth.
2 Beat the cream until stiff; quickly but gently fold papaya into cream (do not overmix). Pour mixture into a shallow 8-inch cake pan. Place in freezer 1 hour or until frozen 1 inch around edge. Stir with a spoon. Return to freezer another 30 minutes to 1 hour or until soft-frozen.
3 To serve: Spoon mixture into reserved papaya shells, dividing evenly (or spoon into sherbet glasses for serving). Garnish with a wedge of lime and reserved papaya balls. Serve at once or return to freezer a few minutes until ready to serve.

Fruit Crown Cheesecake

You'll want to serve this creamy double-tier beauty—large enough for a party—right at the table

Makes 10 servings.

FRUIT MIXTURE

2 envelopes unflavored gelatin
½ cup water
1 can (8 ounces) fruit cocktail
1 tablespoon sugar
1 tablespoon lemon juice
1 teaspoon rum flavoring or extract

CHEESE MIXTURE

2 eggs, separated
½ cup milk
½ cup sugar
1 teaspoon salt
2 cups (1 pound) cream-style cottage cheese
1 teaspoon grated lemon peel
2 tablespoons lemon juice
1 teaspoon vanilla
1 cup cream for whipping

TOPPING

1 banana

1 Make fruit mixture: Soften gelatin in water in top of double boiler; heat, stirring constantly,

Combine fruit with cheese and you have the taste-filled **Fruit Crown Cheesecake—**
a double decker that everyone will enjoy.

over boiling water until gelatin dissolves; remove from heat.

2 Combine fruit cocktail and syrup, sugar, lemon juice and rum flavoring or extract in small bowl; stir in 1 tablespoon of the dissolved gelatin. Pour into an 8-cup mold. Let stand at room temperature until cheese mixture is made.

3 Make cheese mixture: Stir egg yolks, milk, sugar and salt into remaining dissolved gelatin in top of double boiler. Heat, stirring constantly, over simmering water, 10 minutes, or until mixture thickens slightly; cool.

4 Press cottage cheese through sieve into large bowl. (Or beat with electric mixer until creamy-smooth.) Stir in lemon peel, lemon juice, vanilla and cooled gelatin mixture.

5 Chill fruit layer in mold until sticky-firm; chill cheese mixture, stirring several times, until as thick as unbeaten egg white.

6 Beat egg whites until they stand in firm peaks in medium-size bowl. Beat cream until stiff in small bowl.

7 Fold beaten egg whites, then whipped cream into cheese mixture; pour over sticky-firm fruit layer in mold; chill until firm.

8 When ready to serve, loosen mold around edge with a thin-blade knife, then dip *very quickly* in and out of a pan of hot water. Invert onto serving plate; lift off mold.

9 Peel and slice banana; arrange slices, overlapping, in a ring around top; place a cluster of sugared grapes in center, if you wish. (To make: Dip a small bunch of green grapes into

a mixture of 1 egg white beaten slightly with ½ teaspoon water in small bowl, then into granulated sugar, turning to coat grapes well. Let dry on paper toweling.)

Pineapple Chiffon Cake

Another time, make this with a pineapple-and-mint sauce

Bake at 325 degrees for 35 minutes.
Makes one 9-inch ring cake

1 cup sifted cake flour
¾ cups sugar
1 teaspoon baking powder
¼ teaspoon salt
¼ cup vegetable oil
2 eggs, separated
⅓ cup unsweetened pineapple juice
1 teaspoon grated lemon rind (optional)

1 Grease and flour 8-cup ring mold or 9-inch Bundt ® pan.

2 Sift flour, ½ cup sugar, baking powder, and salt into large bowl. Add oil, egg yolks, pineapple juice, and lemon rind; beat with wooden spoon until smooth.

3 Beat egg white in medium size bowl until

(continued)

foamy white and double in volume. Gradually beat in the remaining sugar until meringue stands in soft peaks. Add to yolk mixture; fold in gently. Spoon into prepared pan.

4 Bake in slow oven 325 degrees for 35 minutes or until top springs back when lightly pressed with fingertips.

5 Cool on wire rack ten minutes; loosen around edge with small spatula; ease cake out of pan; cool completely on wire rack.

Melon In Sabayon Sauce

Cool and refreshing honeydew melon balls served with a satin-smooth wine sabayon sauce—a perfect way to finish a summer meal

Makes 6 servings.

½ *teaspoon unflavored gelatin*
¼ *cup sugar*
½ *cup orange juice*
¼ *cup white port wine or dry sherry*
2 *eggs, slightly beaten*
1 *honeydew melon, chilled*

1 Sprinkle gelatin and sugar over orange juice and port wine in large bowl or double boiler; beat in eggs. Set over barely simmering water.

2 Cook, beating constantly with a whisk or rotary hand beater, until mixture thickens slightly and is double in volume, about 8 to 12 minutes. Remove from hot water and set in ice water. Beat mixture until cool, then remove from ice water.

3 Scoop enough melon balls from melon with melon baller to fill 6 dessert glasses; keep refrigerated. Just before serving, pour sauce over each serving.

Plum Sherbet

This light and refreshing plum sherbet can be made in either an ice cream freezer or the freezer section of your refrigerator

Makes about 2 quarts.

2 *pounds red or purple plums*
1⅓ *cups sugar*
1¼ *cups water*
2 *tablespoons lemon juice*
REFRIGERATOR-FREEZER METHOD:
2 *egg whites*
2 *tablespoons sugar*

METHOD FOR ICE CREAM FREEZER:
1 Wash, pit and dice plums (you should have about 4 cups).

2 Combine sugar and water in large saucepan; bring to boiling, stirring constantly until sugar is dissolved. Cook, uncovered, over low heat 5 minutes. Add plums; bring to boiling, stirring often. Remove from heat; stir in lemon juice; cover; cool completely.

3 Lift plums from juice with slotted spoon to container of electric blender. Puree until smooth; return puree to juice.

4 Pour mixture into freezer can; adjust dasher and top. Freeze, using recommended amounts of ice and salt and following manufacturer's directions. Spoon sherbet into plastic containers; cover. Freeze until firm.

METHOD FOR REFRIGERATOR-FREEZER:
Before you begin, make sure freezer is at and will maintain 0°.

1 Follow above recipe through step 3. Pour plum mixture into 9x9x2-inch pan. Place in freezer with the pan touching one of the freezer surfaces. Freeze mixture, stirring several times, until frozen to a mush, about 4 hours. Chill a large bowl.

2 Beat egg whites until foamy white in small bowl; beat in the 2 tablespoons sugar until meringue forms soft peaks.

3 Turn partially frozen mixture into chilled bowl. Beat with electric mixer until very smooth. Fold in meringue, working quickly so mixture does not melt. Spoon into plastic containers; cover. Return to freezer for at least 6 hours.

Carolina Melon Salad

Delicious with the spicy ginger dressing

Makes 6 to 8 servings.

1 Arrange slices of cantaloupe, honeydew and lime, overlapping, in rings in a large bowl.

2 Serve with GINGER DRESSING to spoon over.
GINGER DRESSING
Combine ½ cup honey with ¼ cup orange juice, 2 tablespoons lemon juice and 1 teaspoon ground ginger in a small bowl until well mixed.

Fruit	SPRING AND SUMMER FAVORITES	
	·Season	Shopping Tips
APRICOTS	June and July	Look for plump, juicy apricots of uniform orange-gold color.
BLUEBERRIES	May through September	Choose firm, deep-blue berries with silvery bloom.
CHERRIES (SWEET)	May through August	Select dark, rich red fruits—it's your best guarantee of ripeness *and* sweetness. *Note:* Most sour cherries are sold frozen or canned.
MELONS	Varies with variety.	
NECTARINES	June through September	These are smooth-skinned peaches. Choose those of rich peach-to-rose color, those that are plump and beginning to soften along the seam.
PEACHES	July to September	There are two main types—*freestone* (flesh does not cling to pit) and *clingstone* (flesh *does* cling to pit; these are "canning" peaches).
PLUMS	June to September	Choose firm-soft, fragrant fruits of rich red-to-purple or blue color.
RASPBERRIES, BLACKBERRIES, BOYSENBERRIES, DEWBERRIES	July to September	These differ as to color, size and flavor, but structurally, they're the same. Regardless of species, look for clean bright berries, unbroken, unmoldy with no attached stem caps.
STRAWBERRIES	April to July	Look for rich red berries, plump and firm with cap stems still attached.

Apricot Rice-Pudding Pie

Creamy rice pudding plus juicy golden apricots add up to a double dessert-treat

Bake at 400° for 30 minutes.
Makes one 9-inch pie.

½ cup uncooked regular rice
½ cup sugar
2 tablespoons butter or margarine
¼ teaspoon salt
¼ teaspoon ground allspice
1 cup milk
1 cup water
1 package piecrust mix

1 can (1 pound, 13 ounces) apricot halves, drained
Cream
Sugar

1 Combine rice, sugar, butter or margarine, salt, allspice, milk and water in large saucepan; heat to boiling. Cover; simmer 30 minutes, or until rice is tender but still moist. Remove from heat; save for next step.
2 Prepare piecrust mix, following label directions, or make pastry from your favorite two-crust recipe. Roll out half to a 12-inch round on lightly floured pastry cloth or board; fit into a 9-inch pie plate. Spoon rice mixture into shell; arrange apricot halves, rounded side up, on top.

(continued)

3 Roll out remaining pastry to a 12x8-inch rectangle; brush lightly with cream and sprinkle with sugar; cut into 10 strips, each about ¾ inch wide. Weave strips over filling to make a criss-cross top; trim overhang to ½-inch; turn up over edge and flute.

4 Bake in hot oven (400°) 30 minutes, or until pastry is golden. Cool on wire rack. Serve with cream or a dollop of creamy topping from a pressurized can, if you wish.

Watermelon Ice

An excellent accompaniment at a barbecue

Makes 4 servings.

3 cups chopped watermelon, seeded
2 tablespoons lemon juice
½ cup sugar
1 envelope unflavored gelatin
½ cup water

1 Place watermelon, about half at a time, in an electric-blender container; cover. Beat until smooth and liquid. (There should be about 2 cups.) Pour into a medium-size bowl; stir in lemon juice. (If you do not have a blender, press watermelon through a sieve into a bowl.)

2 Mix sugar and gelatin in a small saucepan; stir in water. Heat slowly, stirring constantly, until gelatin dissolves. Cool slightly; stir into watermelon mixture. Pour into a 9x9x2-inch pan.

3 Freeze about 1½ hours, or until firm around edges.

4 Spoon into a large bowl; beat until smooth; return to pan. Freeze several hours longer, or until firm.

Cantaloupe Cream Melba

It has a delicious berry sauce

Makes 8 servings.

1 package (10 ounces) frozen raspberries thawed
⅔ cup sugar
  Dash cream of tartar
1 large cantaloupe
1 quart peach or vanilla ice cream

1 Press raspberries through a sieve into a small saucepan; stir in sugar and cream of tartar.

2 Heat quickly, stirring constantly, to boiling; cook 3 minutes. Pour into a small bowl; chill.

3 Halve cantaloupe; scoop out seeds; pare melon. Cut each half into 4 wedges.

4 Arrange wedges, spoke fashion and rounded sides down, around edge in a compote or shallow serving bowl; scoop ice cream into balls and pile in center. Drizzle part of the raspberry sauce over ice cream, then serve remainder separately.

Honeydew Horn of Plenty

Refrigerate first and this will be cool and refreshing at a picnic

Makes 6 servings.

2 medium-size honeydew melons
¼ large watermelon
1 can (6 ounces) frozen concentrate for orange juice, thawed
½ cup dry white wine
3 limes

1 Halve one of the honeydew melons; scoop out seeds. Cut out enough balls with a melon-ball cutter or the ½ teaspoon of a measuring-spoon set to make 3 cups; place in a medium-size bowl. Remove seeds from watermelon; cut into balls. (There should be about 3 cups.) Combine with honeydew balls.

2 Pour the orange-juice concentrate and wine over fruit in bowl; toss lightly to mix; cover. Chill at least 4 hours to blend flavors.

3 Just before serving, cut a thin slice diagonally from end of remaining honeydew melon; scoop out seeds with a long-handle spoon. Make a ½-inch-deep cut all around melon just inside rind with a small sharp-tip knife.

4 Slice limes thin; quarter each slice. Push part of the wedges, rind side out, into cut in melon.

5 Place melon at one end of a large serving plate; spoon chilled melon balls into hollow and along plate to resemble a cornucopia. Garnish with remaining lime wedges, and orange wedges, if you wish.

A fast dessert made from a mix, **Royal Fruit Tart** teams cling peaches, canned whole plums with pudding and piecrust mix.

Royal Fruit Tart

Here's a luscious way to butter up both fruit- and cream-pie fans at once

Bake at 400° for 20 minutes.
Makes one 9-inch tart.

1 package piecrust mix
2 tablespoons sugar
1 egg
1 package (about 4 ounces) vanilla-flavor pudding mix
⅛ teaspoon ground nutmeg
1 cup milk
1 small can evaporated milk (⅔ cup)
1 teaspoon vanilla
1 can (about 1 pound) sliced cling peaches
1 tablespoon cornstarch
1 tablespoon lemon juice
1 can (1 pound, 14 ounces) whole purple plums, drained and pitted

1 Combine piecrust mix, sugar and egg in medium-size bowl. Mix with a fork until well blended.
2 Press in bottom and up side of a 9x1½-inch layer-cake pan, making rim flush with edge of pan. (Shell will be thick.) Prick well all over with a fork.
3 Bake in hot oven (400°) 20 minutes, or until golden. Cool on wire rack 10 minutes; carefully invert onto second wire rack; lift off pan Turn shell right side up; cool completely.

4 Combine pudding mix, nutmeg, milk and evaporated milk in small saucepan. Cook, following label directions; stir in vanilla. Pour into small bowl; cover; chill.
5 Drain and measure syrup from peaches to make ¾ cup. Stir a little into cornstarch until smooth in small saucepan, then add remainder. Cook, stirring constantly, until mixture thickens and bubbles 1 minute; stir in lemon juice. Remove from heat, but keep warm.
6 Pour chilled pudding mixture into cooled shell; arrange peach slices and whole plums on top. Spoon warm glaze over. Chill at least 2 hours.

Strawberries Chantilly

Rum sauce complements fresh berries

Makes 4 servings.

4 egg yolks
4 tablespoons sugar
Dash of salt
½ cup milk
½ cup light cream or table cream
1 tablespoon rum flavoring
2 pints (4 cups) strawberries, washed and hulled
10X (confectioners' powdered) sugar

(continued)

1 Beat egg yolks with sugar and salt until light in top of small double boiler. Stir in milk and cream.
2 Cook, stirring constantly, over simmering water, 8 minutes, or until mixture thickens and coats a metal spoon. Strain at once into a medium-size bowl; stir in rum flavoring; cool.
3 When ready to serve, spoon strawberries into sherbet or dessert dishes, dividing evenly. Pour sauce around strawberries; sprinkle lightly with 10X sugar.

Strawberry-Chiffon Tarts

For easier baking, place tart shell pans on a cookie sheet

Bake at 425° for 15 minutes.
Makes 12 tarts.

1 package piecrust mix
1 envelope unflavored gelatin
½ cup sugar
½ cup water
1 cup crushed strawberries (about 1 pint whole)
1 tablespoon lemon juice
1 cup cream for whipping

1 Prepare piecrust mix, following label directions.
2 Roll out half of pastry to ⅛-inch thickness on lightly floured pastry cloth or board; cut out six 6-inch rounds. Fit each into a four-inch tart-shell pan, pressing dough firmly against bottom and side; prick all over with a fork. Repeat with remaining half of pastry.
3 Bake in hot oven (425°) 15 minutes, or until golden; cool completely on wire rack before removing from pans.
4 Combine gelatin and sugar in small saucepan; stir in water. Heat slowly, stirring constantly, 5 minutes, or until gelatin dissolves. Pour over crushed strawberries and lemon juice in medium size bowl; chill until mixture is as thick as unbeaten egg whites.
5 While gelatin mixture chills, beat cream until stiff in small bowl.
6 Place bowl of thickened gelatin mixture in pan of ice and water; beat until fluffy. Fold in whipped cream until no streaks of white remain, then continue folding just until mixture mounds. Remove from bowl of ice at once, as mixture is very cold and will set fast.
7 Spoon quickly into cooled tart shells, using about 4 tablespoonfuls for each; swirl tops with

tip of teaspoon. Chill about 30 minutes. Garnish each with a whole strawberry threaded on a wooden pick, if you wish.

Strawberry Glacé Surprise

Lemon brings out the fresh fruit flavor

Bake at 250° for 40 minutes.
Makes 12 servings.

MERINGUE SHELLS
3 egg whites
½ teaspoon cream of tartar
⅛ teaspoon salt
1 cup sugar
½ teaspoon vanilla

FILLING
¾ cup sugar
3 tablespoons cornstarch
¼ teaspoon salt
3 egg yolks (from meringue shells)
⅓ cup lemon juice
1¼ cups water
1 teaspoon grated lemon peel
2 tablespoons butter or margarine

GLAZE
½ cup strawberry jam
½ cup light corn syrup
2 drops red food coloring
4 cups strawberries, washed and hulled (2 pints)

1 Make meringue shells: Beat egg whites, cream of tartar, and salt until foamy-white and double in volume in medium-size bowl. Beat in sugar, 1 tablespoon at a time, beating well after each, until meringue stands in firm peaks. (Sugar should be completely dissolved before adding more. Beating should take about 10 minutes.) Fold in vanilla.
2 Line a large cookie sheet with brown paper; mark twelve 3-inch circles, 2 inches apart, on paper. Drop meringue, about 4 tablespoonfuls for each, inside circles; spread into rounds with small spatula, building up side of each to form a shell.
3 Bake in very slow oven (250°) 40 minutes, or until crisp. Set cookie sheet on wire rack until meringues cool completely, then remove with spatula. (Shells may be made a day ahead and stored in a container with a tight-fitting cover.)
4 Make filling: Combine sugar, cornstarch and salt in medium-size saucepan. Beat egg yolks slightly in 2-cup measure; stir in lemon juice and water; stir into sugar mixture.

(continued)

In season or out, **Strawberry-Chiffon Tart** (left) and **Strawberries Chantilly** (right) will satisfy strawberry-lovers.

5 Cook over medium heat, stirring constantly, until mixture thickens and bubbles 3 minutes. Remove from heat; stir in lemon peel and butter or margarine; cool.

6 When ready to fill shells, make glaze: Combine jam, corn syrup and red food coloring in small saucepan; heat, stirring constantly, just until hot; remove from heat.

7 To fill shells, spoon about 2 tablespoons filling into each; top with 6 whole strawberries, standing each tip end up; spoon about 1 tablespoon warm glaze over. (Shells may be filled about an hour before serving time, if you like, then chilled.)

Strawberries Parisienne

Pumpkin-pie spice and strawberries combine in this French dessert

Makes 6 servings.

1 package (3 or 4 ounces) cream cheese
1 cup dairy sour cream
1 tablespoon sugar
¼ teaspoon pumpkin-pie spice
2 cups sweetened sliced strawberries (about 1½ pints whole)

1 Soften cream cheese in small bowl, then beat until fluffy. Stir in sour cream, sugar and pumpkin-pie spice until well blended.

2 Spoon alternate layers of cream-cheese mixture and strawberries into six parfait or juice glasses, dividing evenly. Garnish each with a sprig of fresh mint, if you like.

Strawberry-Rhubarb Shortcake

A favorite fruit combination

Bake at 450° for 20 minutes.
Makes 8 servings.

1 pound rhubarb
1¾ cups granulated sugar
2 tablespoons water
1 pint strawberries (2 cups)
2 cups sifted all-purpose flour
3 teaspoons baking powder
½ teaspoon salt
5 tablespoons butter or margarine
¼ cup vegetable shortening
1 egg

⅓ cup milk
1 cup cream for whipping
2 tablespoons 10X (confectioners' powdered) sugar

1 Wash rhubarb, trim ends and cut in 1-inch pieces. (There should be about 3 cups.)

2 Combine with ¾ cup of the granulated sugar and water in a medium-size heavy saucepan; cover. Heat over low heat to boiling, then simmer 5 minutes, or until tender; remove from heat. Set aside to cool. (Rhubarb will finish cooking in heat from pan.)

3 Wash strawberries, hull and slice into a medium-size bowl; sprinkle with ½ cup of the remaining granulated sugar; set aside while making shortcake.

4 Sift flour, remaining ½ cup granulated sugar, baking powder and salt into a medium-size bowl; cut in 4 tablespoons of the butter or margarine and shortening with a pastry blender until mixture is crumbly.

5 Beat egg slightly with milk in a small bowl; add all at once to flour mixture; stir with a fork until evenly moist. Turn out onto a lightly floured pastry cloth or board; knead gently ½ minute. Pat into a greased 8-inch layer-cake pan.

6 Melt remaining 1 tablespoon butter or margarine in a small frying pan; brush over dough; sprinkle lightly with granulated sugar, if you wish.

7 Bake in very hot oven (450°) 20 minutes, or until golden. Cool in pan on a wire rack 5 minutes; turn out onto rack.

8 Beat cream with 10X sugar until stiff in a medium-size bowl.

9 Split warm shortcake with a sharp knife; place bottom layer on a serving plate. Top with half each of the rhubarb, strawberries and cream; cover with remaining shortcake layer, fruit and cream.

10 Cut into wedges with a sharp knife; serve warm.

Devonshire Apple Pie

The crumble topping adds to the pie's flavor and appearance

Bake at 350° for 40 minutes.
Makes one 9-inch pie.

½ package piecrust mix
¾ cup granulated sugar
¾ cup firmly packed brown sugar
2 tablespoons all-purpose flour (for filling)

1 teaspoon ground cinnamon
¼ teaspoon ground nutmeg
1 teaspoon lemon juice
¾ cup dairy sour cream
6 medium-size tart cooking apples, pared,
   quartered, cored and sliced (6 cups)
½ cup sifted all-purpose flour (for topping)
¼ cup (½ stick) butter or margarine
   Process Cheddar cheese

1 Prepare piecrust mix, following label directions, or make pastry from your favorite single-crust recipe. Roll out to a 12-inch round on a lightly floured pastry cloth or board; fit into a 9-inch pie plate. Trim overhang to ½ inch; turn edge under, flush with rim; flute to make a stand-up edge. Set trimmings aside.
2 Mix granulated sugar, ¼ cup of the brown sugar, the 2 tablespoons flour, cinnamon, nutmeg, lemon juice and sour cream in a large bowl; stir in apples. Spoon into prepared pastry shell.
3 Mix the ½ cup flour and remaining ½ cup brown sugar in a small bowl; cut in butter or margarine with a pastry blender until mixture is crumbly. Sprinkle over apple filling.
4 Bake in moderate oven (350°) 40 minutes, or until apples are tender and topping is golden. Cool on a wire rack.
5 Reroll pastry trimmings; cut out six small leaf shapes with a knife or truffle cutter. Place on a cookie sheet; prick with a fork. Bake in same oven with pie 10 minutes, or until golden. Cool.
6 Shape three tiny "apples" from cheese; stick a whole clove in each for a stem. Just before serving, arrange a cheese apple between each two pastry leaves on top of pie.

Butterscotch Apple Cake

Cinnamon candies add zing to apple upside-down cake

Bake at 350° for 45 minutes.
Makes 12 servings.

2 large baking apples
¼ cup red cinnamon candies
   Water
½ cup (1 stick) butter or margarine
1 cup firmly packed light brown sugar
8 maraschino cherries
⅓ cup chopped pecans
1 package yellow cake mix
   Eggs
   Whipped cream

1 Core apples, but do not pare; cut each in 4 thick rings.
2 Combine cinnamon candies and ½ cup water in a large frying pan. Heat, stirring constantly, until candies melt; add apple rings. Simmer, turning once, 3 minutes; remove with a slotted spoon and drain on paper toweling.
3 Melt butter or margarine in a 13x9x2-inch baking pan; stir in brown sugar. Place apple rings in two rows over sugar mixture; top each with a maraschino cherry; sprinkle pecans between apples.
4 Prepare cake mix with eggs and water, following label directions; pour evenly over apples in pan.
5 Bake in moderate oven (350°) 45 minutes, or until golden and top springs back when lightly pressed with fingertip. Cool in pan on a wire rack 10 minutes. Loosen around edges with a knife; invert onto a large serving plate. Let stand 5 minutes; carefully lift off pan. Serve warm with whipped cream.

Apple Dumplings with Raspberry Sauce

They're filled with brown sugar, cinnamon, and butter

Bake at 425° for 35 minutes.
Makes 6 servings.

6 medium-size baking apples
¼ cup (½ stick) butter or margarine
1 cup firmly packed brown sugar
1 teaspoon ground cinnamon
1 package piecrust mix
1 egg, beaten
   RASPBERRY SAUCE (recipe follows)

1 Pare apples and core.
2 Cream butter or margarine with brown sugar and cinnamon until smooth and pastelike in a small bowl. Spoon into hollows in apples, dividing evenly.
3 Prepare piecrust mix, following label directions, or make pastry from your favorite double-crust recipe; divide into 6 equal parts.
4 Roll out, one at a time, to an 8-inch circle on a lightly floured pastry cloth or board; place filled apple in center. Press pastry firmly around apple, folding underneath; trim any excess. Place on a cookie sheet; brush with part of the beaten egg.
5 Roll out pastry trimmings to a rectangle ⅛

(continued)

Three elegant desserts (left to right): **Apple Dumplings, Butterscotch Apple Cake,** and **Devonshire Apple Pie.**

inch thick; cut into long thin strips with a pastry wheel or knife. Press two strips, crisscross fashion, around each dumpling. (Use any remaining pastry trimmings to make small bows on top, if you wish.) Brush strips with beaten egg.

6 Bake in hot oven (425°) 35 minutes, or until apples are tender and pastry is golden. Remove from cookie sheet to a wire rack; serve warm or cold with RASPBERRY SAUCE.

RASPBERRY SAUCE

Thaw 1 package (10 ounces) frozen red raspberries, following label directions. Mix 1 tablespoon cornstarch and 1 tablespoon sugar in a small saucepan; stir in ⅓ cup water and raspberries and syrup. Cook, stirring constantly, until mixture thickens and bubbles 1 minute. Press through a sieve into a small bowl; cool. Makes about 1 cup.

Stuffed Baked Apples

Serve this with your next turkey dinner

Bake at 350° for 1 hour.
Makes 6 servings.

6 large baking apples
½ cup firmly packed brown sugar
½ cup golden raisins
½ teaspoon ground cinnamon
¾ cup honey
½ cup water
1 tablespoon butter or margarine
1 teaspoon grated lemon peel

1 Wash apples and core, then pare about one third of the way down from stem end; stand in shallow 13x9x2-inch baking dish.
2 Mix brown sugar, raisins and cinnamon in a small bowl; spoon into centers of apples, packing down well.
3 Bake in moderate oven (350°), basting often with syrup in dish, 1 hour, or until apples are tender but still firm enough to hold their shape.
4 Cool in dish on a wire rack, spooning syrup over apples often to make a rich glaze.

Molded Grape Compote

Wonderful for a buffet

Makes 8 to 10 servings.

3 envelopes unflavored gelatin
1¼ cups sugar
5½ cups water
1 cup lemon juice
3 large seedless oranges, peeled and sectioned (1½ cups)
1 cup seedless green grapes, halved and seeded
1 large seedless grapefruit, peeled and sectioned (1 cup)
¼ cup flaked coconut

1 Mix gelatin and sugar in a small saucepan; stir in 3½ cups of the water. Heat slowly, stirring constantly, until gelatin dissolves; stir into remaining 2 cups water and lemon juice in a medium-size bowl. Chill while preparing fruits.
2 Measure 2¼ cups of the gelatin mixture into a second medium-size bowl. Place bowl in a pan of ice and water to speed setting; chill until as thick as unbeaten egg white. Fold in orange sections; spoon into an 8-cup serving bowl. Chill in refrigerator.
3 Repeat Step 2, chilling half of the remaining gelatin mixture at a time and folding grapes into one half and grapefruit into the other. Spoon grape mixture over orange layer and grapefruit mixture on top. Chill until firm.
4 Just before serving, spoon coconut in a mound in center of dessert; garnish with a small cluster of green grapes, if you wish.

Triple Fruit Flan

A trio of fresh fruits combine to perfection in this rich delight

Bake at 375° for 15 minutes.
Makes 8 to 10 servings.

1 package piecrust mix
1 egg, beaten
2 tablespoons sugar (for pastry)
1 package (8 ounces) cream cheese
¼ cup sugar (for filling)
1 teaspoon grated lemon peel
2 tablespoons lemon juice
8 fresh plums, halved and pitted
3 cups sliced fresh peaches
1½ cups seedless green grapes (about 1 pound)
½ cup strawberry jelly

(continued)

If you don't have to count the calories, serve **Triple Fruit Flan,** a non-dieter's delight.

1 To make the flan pastry: Fold a 30-inch length of 18-inch-wide heavy-duty aluminum foil in half lengthwise, then in half crosswise, to make a 15x9-inch rectangle.
2 Blend piecrust mix, egg and the 2 tablespoons sugar until mixture leaves side of bowl clean.
3 Pat pastry onto foil rectangle to cover evenly. Turn up edges of foil with pastry to make a 1-inch rim on all sides, squaring off corners and pressing the extra pastry into corners to make a smooth edge. Prick well with fork. Freeze flan crust 2 hours.
4 Bake in moderate oven (375°) 15 minutes, or until golden. Cool completely in foil pan, then remove from foil to serving plate.
5 Blend cream cheese and the ¼ cup sugar until smooth in a small bowl; stir in lemon peel and juice. Spread mixture in bottom of pastry.
6 Arrange fruits in a pretty pattern over cheese layer. Melt jelly in a small saucepan. Brush over fruits. Chill till serving.

Apple-Raisin Crisp

So welcome on a winter evening

Bake at 375° for 45 minutes.
Makes 6 servings.

4 medium-size tart cooking apples
½ cup raisins
¾ cup firmly packed brown sugar
1 teaspoon cinnamon
⅛ teaspoon salt
½ cup (1 stick) butter or margarine
4 cups slightly dry small bread cubes (about 8 slices)
½ cup water

1 Pare, quarter, core and dice apples into a medium-size bowl; mix in raisins, brown sugar; cinnamon and salt.
2 Melt butter or margarine in 6-cup baking dish; stir in bread cubes, tossing lightly. Stir in apple mixture; drizzle water over; cover.
3 Bake in moderate oven (375°) 30 minutes; uncover; bake 15 minutes longer, or until apples are tender and top is browned. Serve warm, plain or with milk, cream or ice cream.

Applesauce Cobbler Cake

Using applesauce cuts preparation time

Bake at 400° for 35 minutes.
Makes 6 servings.

6 tablespoons (¾ stick) butter or margarine
⅓ cup firmly packed brown sugar
½ cup applesauce
1 tablespoon corn syrup
½ teaspoon cinnamon
2 cups sifted all-purpose flour
¼ cup granulated sugar
3 teaspoons baking powder
1 teaspoon salt
⅓ cup vegetable shortening
1 egg
½ cup milk

1 Cream butter or margarine with brown sugar until fluffy in small bowl; stir in applesauce, corn syrup and cinnamon until well blended. Set aside for topping in Step 3.
2 Sift flour, granulated sugar, baking powder and salt into medium-size bowl; cut in shortening with pastry blender until mixture is crumbly.
3 Beat egg with milk until blended in small bowl; pour over flour mixture; stir just until blended. Drop by tablespoonfuls into a greased 9-inch round layer-cake pan. Spoon applesauce topping over dough.
4 Bake in hot oven (400°) 35 minutes, or until cobbler cake starts to pull away from side of pan. Break apart into wedges with two forks. Serve warm with cream, sweetened whipped cream or ice cream, if you wish.

Lemon Dream Pie

Meringue makes the crust for a rich lemon filling

Bake shell at 275° for 1 hour.
Makes one 9-inch pie.

4 eggs, separated
¼ teaspoon cream of tartar
½ teaspoon salt
½ teaspoon vanilla
2 cups sugar
4 tablespoons cornstarch
1½ cups water
½ cup lemon juice
2 tablespoons butter or margarine
1 cup cream for whipping

1 Generously butter a 9-inch pie plate.
2 Beat egg whites with cream of tartar, ¼ teaspoon of the salt, and vanilla until foamy-white and double in volume in a large bowl. Beat in 1 cup of the sugar, 1 tablespoon at a time, beating all the time until sugar dissolves completely and meringue stands in firm peaks. (Beating will take about 25 minutes in all with an electric beater.)
3 Spoon meringue into pie plate. Spread almost to side of plate, hollowing center and building up edge slightly to form a shell.
4 Bake in very slow oven (275°) 1 hour, or until firm and lightly golden. Cool completely in pie plate on a wire rack.
5 While shell bakes, mix remaining 1 cup sugar, cornstarch and ¼ teaspoon salt in a medium-size saucepan. Stir in water, then beat in egg yolks and lemon juice.
6 Cook, stirring constantly, until mixture thickens and bubbles 1 minute; remove from heat. Stir in butter or margarine until melted; pour into a medium-size bowl; cover. Chill until completely cold.
7 Beat cream until stiff in a medium-size bowl. Layer lemon filling, alternately with whipped cream, into meringue shell. Chill about 12 hours before cutting. (To match design on pictured pie, layer about three fourths of the lemon filling and cream into shell. Attach a plain tip to a pastry bag; spoon remaining lemon filling into bag; press out in rings on top of pie. Repeat with whipped cream, filling in spaces between lemon rings.)

Sugared Lemon Crown

Rich as a pound cake, with a hint of lemon; try it with lemon sherbet

Bake at 350° for 50 minutes.
Makes one 9-inch cake.

2¼ cups sifted cake flour
1 teaspoon baking powder
½ teaspoon salt
¾ cup (1½ sticks) butter or margarine
1½ cups granulated sugar
3 eggs
1 tablespoon grated lemon peel
2 tablespoons lemon juice
⅔ cup milk
10X (confectioners' powdered) sugar

1 Butter an 8-cup tube mold; dust lightly with flour, gently tapping out any excess.

(continued)

2 Sift flour, baking powder and salt onto wax paper.

3 Combine butter or margarine, granulated sugar and eggs in large bowl of electric mixer; beat at high speed 3 minutes. (Do not underbeat.) Slowly beat in lemon peel and lemon juice.

4 Add flour mixture, a third at a time, alternately with milk, beating at low speed just until blended. Scrape bowl often between additions. Pour into prepared pan.

5 Bake in moderate oven (350°) 50 minutes, or until top springs back when lightly pressed with fingertip.

6 Cool cake in mold on a wire rack 10 minutes. Loosen around edge with a knife; invert onto rack; cool completely. Before serving, sprinkle lightly with 10X sugar.

Lemon Blossom Tart

The lemon custard is rich, but tangy

Bake shell at 400° for 20 minutes.
Makes 8 servings.

1 package piecrust mix
2 tablespoons sugar (for pastry)
4 eggs
½ cup sugar (for filling)
2 teaspoons grated lemon peel
¼ cup lemon juice
¼ cup (½ stick) butter or margarine
1 cup cream for whipping

1 Combine piecrust mix, the 2 tablespoons sugar and 1 of the eggs in a medium-size bowl. Mix with a fork until well blended.

2 Press evenly over bottom and up side of a 9-inch round layer-cake pan, making rim even with edge of pan. (Shell will be thick.) Prick well all over with a fork.

3 Bake in hot oven (400°) 20 minutes, or until golden. Cool completely in pan on a wire rack.

4 Beat remaining 3 eggs slightly in the top of a double boiler; stir in the ½ cup sugar, lemon peel and juice and butter or margarine. Cook, stirring constantly, over hot (not boiling) water 10 minutes, or until very thick. Pour into a medium-size bowl; chill until completely cold.

5 Beat cream until stiff in a medium-size bowl; fold into lemon custard.

6 Remove pastry shell carefully from pan; place on a large serving plate; spoon lemon filling into shell. Garnish with a pinwheel of candied lemon slices, if you wish. Chill 1 to 2 hours before serving.

Banana Split Pie

The All-American dessert, in an edible container

Bake shell at 425° for 12 minutes.
Makes one 9-inch pie.

½ package piecrust mix
1 pint vanilla ice cream
4 firm ripe bananas
½ cup fudge sundae sauce
2 pints strawberry ice cream
½ cup cream for whipping
½ cup strawberry sundae sauce

1 Prepare piecrust mix, following label directions, or make pastry from your favorite single-crust recipe. Roll out to a 12-inch round on a lightly floured pastry cloth or board; fit into a 9-inch pie plate. Trim overhang to ½ inch; turn under, flush with rim; flute to make a stand-up edge. Prick shell well all over with a fork.

2 Bake in hot oven (425°) 12 minutes, or until golden. Cool completely in pie plate on a wire rack.

3 About an hour before serving, chill pie shell thoroughly in freezer, then spoon in vanilla ice cream to make an even layer. Peel 2 of the bananas; halve each lengthwise and crosswise. Arrange, spoke fashion, over ice cream in shell; spoon fudge sauce over top. Return to freezer.

4 Scoop 8 small balls from part of the strawberry ice cream; place in a shallow pan; freeze firm. Spoon remaining strawberry ice cream into shell; return to freezer.

5 Just before serving, beat cream until stiff in a small bowl. Peel remaining 2 bananas; halve lengthwise and crosswise; arrange over strawberry ice cream. Top with ice-cream balls; spoon strawberry sauce, then whipped cream into center. Cut into wedges.

An always fruit favorite, lemon is the base for these three lovely desserts: **Lemon Blossom Tart** (left), **Sugared Lemon Crown** (top), and **Lemon Dream Pie.**

Ice cream forms the base for many frozen desserts. And what better than ice cream balls drizzled with a rich chocolate sauce.

Frozen Dessert Sensations

Ice creams, ices, bombes, Alaskas, parfaits . . . are examples of frozen desserts that you'll discover in these pages. And each one is guaranteed to make you want to freeze another.

Hot Fudge Sundaes

Rich and satisfying

Makes 4 to 6 servings.

1 quart vanilla ice cream
1 recipe HOT FUDGE SAUCE *(see recipe index for page number)*
½ cup chopped pecans or walnuts (optional)

1 Using a No. 30 ice cream scoop or shaping ice cream into balls with two teaspoons, pile 4 to 5 small balls of ice cream in each of 4 to 6 dessert dishes.
2 Ladle HOT FUDGE SAUCE on top and, if you like, sprinkle with chopped pecans or walnuts.

Regal Rio Sundaes

Double chocolate and doubly rich—that's what these easy-make sundae splurges are

Count on 1 quart of ice cream for 6 to 8 servings. Scoop into dessert dishes; pour warm RIO CHOCOLATE SAUCE over; stand a CHOCOLATE FAN on top of each. *(Recipes follow.)*

Rio Chocolate Sauce

Makes 2 cups.

1 cup (6-ounce package) semisweet-chocolate pieces
¼ cup (½ stick) butter or margarine
1 cup sifted 10X (confectioners' powdered) sugar
½ cup light corn syrup
1 teaspoon instant coffee powder
Dash of salt
½ cup hot water
1 teaspoon vanilla

1 Melt chocolate pieces with butter or margarine in top of double boiler over simmering water. Beat in remaining ingredients until smooth and slightly thickened. Remove from heat.
2 Serve warm or cold over ice cream or pudding or cake desserts. (Make enough to keep on hand, as it stays creamy-smooth stored in a covered jar in the refrigerator. To reheat, set jar, covered, in a pan of simmering water; heat slowly for 10 to 15 minutes.)

VARIATIONS

Double Fudge Sundaes—Prepare as directed for HOT FUDGE SUNDAES *but substitute chocolate ice cream for vanilla.*
Mocha Fudge Sundaes—Prepare as directed for HOT FUDGE SUNDAES *but substitute coffee ice cream for vanilla.*
Berry Fudge Sundaes—Prepare as directed for HOT FUDGE SUNDAES *but substitute strawberry or raspberry ice cream for vanilla.*
Cherry Fudge Sundaes—Prepare as directed for HOT FUDGE SUNDAES *but substitute cherry ice cream for vanilla.*
Chocolate Mint Sundaes—Prepare as directed for HOT FUDGE SUNDAES *but substitute peppermint or mint ice cream for vanilla.*

Brownie Sundae Shortcakes

Brownie dough-in-a-roll from the dairy case stars in this quick dessert

Makes 6 servings.

1 roll refrigerated fudge brownies
2 pints chocolate-ripple ice cream
Creamy topping from a pressurized can

1 Press fudge brownies in a 8x8x2-inch baking pan, following label directions.
2 Cut brownies into 12 bars.
3 Put each 2 together with ice cream between on a serving plate; top with creamy topping from a pressurized can.

Kona Sundaes

Perfect for coffee lovers

Makes 8 servings.

¾ cup firmly packed light brown sugar
1 tablespoon instant coffee powder
  Dash of salt
½ cup water
1 can (15 ounces) sweetened condensed milk
  (not evaporated)
3 pints vanilla or coffee ice cream

1 Mix brown sugar, instant coffee, salt and water in medium-size heavy saucepan; heat, stirring constantly, to boiling, then cook, without stirring, to 230° on a candy thermometer. (A little syrup will spin fine threads when dropped from tip of spoon.) Remove from heat.
2 Place sweetened condensed milk in medium-size bowl; blend in hot syrup slowly; cool.
3 When ready to serve, scoop ice cream into dessert dishes, dividing evenly; spoon sauce over.

Coffee-Almond Sparkle Sundaes

Topped with a shimmery sauce and toasted nuts

Makes 6 servings.

2 cups firmly packed brown sugar
¼ cup dark corn syrup
3 tablespoons water
1 tablespoon lemon juice
¾ teaspoon salt
1 tablespoon butter or margarine
1 teaspoon vanilla
2 pints coffee ice cream
¼ cup toasted blanched almonds

1 Mix sugar, corn syrup, water, lemon juice and salt in medium-size saucepan. Heat slowly, stirring just until sugar dissolves; add butter or margarine.
2 Heat to boiling; cook, without stirring, to 230° on candy thermometer. (A little syrup will spin fine threads when dropped from tip of spoon.)
3 Remove from heat; stir in vanilla; cool.
4 Scoop ice cream into dessert dishes; spoon sauce over; top with almonds.

Sinker Sundaes

Peanut butter makes the sauce, doughnuts are the cake

Makes 6 servings.

½ cup crunchy peanut butter
½ cup light corn syrup
¼ cup water
6 plain doughnuts
1 pint vanilla ice cream

1 Combine peanut butter with corn syrup and water in a small saucepan; heat slowly, stirring constantly, until well blended; cool.
2 For each sundae, place a doughnut in a serving dish; top with ice cream; drizzle with warm peanut sauce.

Quick Butterscotch Sundaes

Evaporated milk gives smooth results in a jiffy

Makes 6 servings.

1½ cups firmly packed light brown sugar
½ cup light corn syrup
1 tablespoon butter or margarine
1 small can (⅔ cup) evaporated milk
½ teaspoon vanilla
1 quart vanilla ice cream

1 Boil brown sugar and corn syrup, stirring often, 5 minutes. Add butter or margarine, pour into a bowl and cool 10 minutes.
2 Slowly stir in evaporated milk and vanilla. Spoon warm over vanilla ice cream.

Honey-Butter Sundaes

Next time, serve the sauce over frozen yogurt

Makes 4 servings.

½ cup honey
1 tablespoon butter or margarine
3 tablespoons orange juice
½ teaspoon vanilla
¼ teaspoon almond extract
1 quart vanilla ice cream

1 Heat honey, butter or margarine and orange juice in a small saucepan about 5 minutes, stirring often.

2 Remove from heat, stir in vanilla and almond extract. Cool about 5 minutes; spoon warm over vanilla ice cream.

Bunny Sundaes

A nice Easter dessert for the children

Makes 4 servings.

½ pound caramel-candy cubes
½ cup evaporated milk
4 marshmallows
   Red food coloring
8 small red gumdrops
1 pint coffee ice cream

1 Melt caramels in milk over hot water, stirring often to blend.
2 Draw bunny face on marshmallows with wooden pick and food coloring; attach gumdrop "ears" with picks.
3 Spoon caramel sauce over each serving of ice cream; top with marshmallow bunny.

Calypso Sundaes

A taste of the West Indies, to enliven any dinner

Makes 8 servings.

1 can (about 1 pound) pear halves, drained
1 can (8 ounces) crushed pineapple
½ cup mint jelly
1 teaspoon lemon juice
2 pints lemon sherbet
   Maraschino cherries

1 Break up pear halves with spoon in me-dium-size saucepan; add pineapple and juice and mint jelly; simmer 10 minutes, or until blended and slightly thickened; add lemon juice; chill.
2 Spoon over sherbet in serving dishes; top with maraschino cherries.

A quick-fix dessert, **Jubilee Sundae Stacks** are made in a jiffy.

Jubilee Sundae Stacks

Celebration fare at a moment's notice!

Makes 4 servings.

4 packaged dessert shells
1 pint vanilla ice cream
1 package (10 ounces) quick-thaw frozen dark
   sweet cherries

Place each dessert shell on a serving plate; top with a scoop of ice cream; spoon cherries over all.

Peach Fiesta Splits

Try this with frozen cherries, too

Makes 6 servings.

1 package (10 ounces) frozen sliced peaches
½ teaspoon almond extract
1 pint vanilla ice cream
1 pint pistachio ice cream

(continued)

1 Thaw peaches in a small bowl; stir in almond extract.
2 Scoop out vanilla and pistachio ice creams, dividing evenly among 6 dessert dishes. Spoon peaches on top.

Pear Splits

A pleasant change from banana

Makes 6 servings.

12 canned pear halves
 1 quart vanilla ice cream

 1 recipe FAST FUDGE SAUCE (see recipe index
   for page number)
 ½ cup chopped salted peanuts

Arrange 2 pear halves in each of 6 dessert dishes. Place scoops of ice cream between pear halves, top with FAST FUDGE SAUCE and chopped peanuts

Peppermint Snowballs

It has a translucent green topping

Makes 6 servings.

 2 pints lemon sherbet
 ½ cup light corn syrup
 1½ teaspoons peppermint extract
   Green food coloring

1 Scoop lemon sherbet into balls with a small ice-cream scoop or shape with two spoons. Place on cookie sheet; cover loosely with wax paper, transparent wrap or foil; freeze until serving time.
2 Mix corn syrup and peppermint extract in a 1-cup measure; tint delicate green with food coloring.
3 When ready to serve, pile sherbet balls into a pretty glass serving bowl; drizzle sauce over.

In the middle of the summer heat, try **Peppermint Snowballs.** Grown-ups as well as kids will enjoy the icy-cold dessert.

Chocolate Mint Parfaits

Creamy mint-flavored parfait mixture complemented by chocolate sauce is a treat that is unbelievably easy to make

Makes 6 servings.

1 pint vanilla ice cream
1 package (3 ounces) whipped topping mix
  Milk

1 envelope unflavored gelatin
⅓ cup water
1 teaspoon peppermint extract
  Green food coloring
½ cup bottled or canned chocolate sauce

1 Spoon ice cream into a large bowl and let stand at room temperature about 15 minutes, or until slightly softened.
2 Prepare topping mix with milk in a medium-size bowl, following label directions. Reserve ½ cup for garnish in Step 6.
3 Soften gelatin in water in a small saucepan, dissolve over low heat, stirring constantly; remove from heat.
4 With electric mixer, beat ice cream until smooth in a medium-size bowl; add peppermint extract and enough food coloring to tint a delicate green; fold in whipped topping. Add the hot gelatin all at once, beating in quickly and constantly, until mixture is smooth.
5 Layer mint mixture alternately with chocolate sauce into 6 parfait glasses.
6 Garnish each serving with reserved topping. Serve immediately or chill until serving time. Top with a sprig of fresh mint, if you wish.

Paradise Parfaits

Refreshing after a Chinese dinner

Makes 8 servings.

2 cups diced cantaloupe ·
1 cup red raspberries or sliced strawberries
3 pints strawberry ice cream
1 cup cream, whipped
4 peaches, peeled, halved and pitted

1 Layer fruits and ice cream, dividing evenly, into stemmed glasses this way: Cantaloupe, raspberries or strawberries, ice cream. Top each with whipped cream, then with a peach half.
2 Stick a perky Oriental paper parasol or lantern into each peach half, if you wish.

Dublin Ice-Cream Bombe

Like frozen Irish coffee

Makes 10 servings.

1 quart coffee ice cream
1 quart vanilla ice cream

½ cup Irish Mist liqueur
1 teaspoon almond extract

1 Lightly butter an 8-cup bombe mold. Line mold with foil, leaving a 2-inch overhang all around; press foil smoothly against side of mold.
2 Soften coffee ice cream slightly in a medium-size bowl. Spoon into mold, smoothing over bottom and up side to make a shell about 1 inch thick. Freeze until firm.
3 Soften vanilla ice cream slightly in a medium-size bowl. Beat in liqueur and almond extract; spoon into center of mold; smooth top flat. Fold foil over top. Freeze several hours, or overnight, until very firm.
4 When ready to serve, peel back foil from top of mold. Pull up on foil to loosen around edge. Invert onto a serving plate; peel off foil. Garnish with almonds, if you wish. Cut into slices with a sharp knife.

Hazelnut Cream Bombe

Substitute almonds for the hazelnuts, if you wish

Makes 12 to 16 servings.

1 tablespoon butter or margarine
1 cup chopped hazelnuts or filberts
¼ cup candied green cherries, chopped
1½ pints vanilla ice cream, slightly softened
1 pint chocolate ice cream, slightly softened
1½ cups sugar
½ cup water
4 egg yolks
2 tablespoons light rum
3 cups cream for whipping

1 Melt butter or margarine in a shallow pan; sprinkle hazelnuts into pan, tossing to coat with butter. Toast in moderate oven (350°), stirring several times, 10 minutes, or until richly golden. Cool and set aside.
2 Lightly butter a 10-cup mixing bowl. Line with foil, pressing foil smooth against side and leaving a 2-inch overhang all around.
3 Stir cherries into vanilla ice cream in a medium-size bowl; spoon into foil-lined mold, shaping around edge to leave a hollow in middle. Freeze 2 hours, or until firm. Repeat with chocolate ice cream to make a thin middle layer; freeze.
4 While chocolate ice cream freezes, combine sugar and water in a medium-size saucepan. Cook rapidly to 236° on a candy thermometer.

(continued)

(A teaspoonful of syrup will form a soft ball when dropped in cold water.)

5 Beat egg yolks until fluffy-light in a medium-size bowl; slowly pour in syrup in a fine stream, beating constantly at high speed until mixture is very light and thick. Cool slightly; beat in rum. Chill until completely cold.

6 Beat 2 cups of the cream until stiff in a medium-size bowl; fold into chilled egg mixture; fold in hazelnuts. Spoon into hollow in ice-cream mold; fold foil over top to cover. Freeze at least 6 hours, or overnight.

7 When ready to unmold, beat remaining 1 cup cream until stiff in a medium-size bowl.

8 Peel foil from top of mold; loosen around edge with a knife and pull up on foil to loosen from bowl. Invert onto a serving plate; peel off foil. Attach a rosette tip to a pastry bag; spoon whipped cream into bag. Press out in rows of rosettes, spoke fashion, around mold. To serve, cut in wedges.

Walnut Bombe Alaska

Bake cake at 350° for 30 minutes,
meringue at 475° for 3 to 4 minutes.
Makes 12 servings.

ICE-CREAM MOLD

2 pints coffee ice cream, slightly softened
1 pint strawberry ice cream, slightly softened

TORTE LAYER

1 cup sifted all-purpose flour
2 teaspoons baking powder
⅛ teaspoon salt
½ cup vegetable shortening
½ cup firmly packed brown sugar
4 egg yolks
⅓ cup milk
½ teaspoon vanilla
1 cup chopped walnuts

MERINGUE FROSTING

4 egg whites
¼ teaspoon cream of tartar
½ cup sugar

1 Make ice-cream mold: Line an 8-cup melon mold or mixing bowl with foil, pressing it into the mold shape and leaving a 1-inch overhang all around. Spoon coffee ice cream into mold, spreading evenly over bottom and up side to line completely and leave a hollow in middle for strawberry ice cream. Freeze until firm, then spoon strawberry ice cream into hollow. Smooth top flat with a knife; cover. Freeze several hours, overnight, or until very firm.

2 Make torte layer: Measure flour, baking powder and salt into sifter.

3 Cream shortening with brown sugar until fluffy in a medium-size bowl; beat in egg yolks, 1 at a time, beating well after each addition until mixture is well blended.

4 Sift in dry ingredients, a third at a time, adding alternately with milk; stir just until blended, then stir in vanilla and walnuts. Pour into a greased and floured 9x1½-inch layer-cake pan.

5 Bake in moderate oven (350°) 30 minutes, or until top springs back when lightly pressed with fingertip.

6 Cool in pan on wire rack 5 minutes. Loosen around edge with knife; turn out onto rack; cool completely

7 Put Alaska together this way: Place torte layer on a double-thick strip of foil on a cookie sheet. (This makes it easy to slide hot dessert onto its serving plate.) Loosen ice cream from mold by lifting up overhanging tabs of foil, then invert onto center of torte layer. Lift off mold; peel off foil. Trim torte layer to within ¼ inch of ice-cream mold. Return to freezer until ready to frost with meringue, bake, and serve.

8 Make meringue: Beat egg whites with cream of tartar until foamy-white and double in volume in a medium-size bowl. Sprinkle in granulated sugar *very slowly,* 1 tablespoon at a time, beating all the time until sugar completely dissolves and meringue stands in firm peaks. (Beating will take about 20 minutes in all.)

9 Spread over ice-cream-cake mold, swirling in peaks, to cover completely. (Work quickly so the ice cream doesn't melt.)

10 Bake in very hot oven (475°) 3 to 4 minutes, or just until peaks are toasty-golden.

11 Slide Alaska onto a chilled serving plate; pull out foil strip. Use a sharp bread or carving knife to slice or cut into wedges.

Note: To avoid last-minute fussing, you can frost ice-cream-cake mold with meringue ahead, then return to freezer. Just before serving, slide in to bake, following directions in Step 10 above.

Mexican Cream Torte

Packaged cookies are the cake base in this ice cream treat

Makes 6 to 8 generous servings.

1 package (about 7 ounces) coconut cookies
3 pints chocolate ice cream, softened slightly
¾ cup chocolate syrup
1 pint orange sherbet, softened slightly
1 cup crushed peanut brittle

Two ice creams atop a walnut cake, make **Walnut Bombe Alaska** a festive version of the "fire and ice" classic.

1 Crush cookies fine with a rolling pin. (There should be 2 cups crumbs.) Sprinkle about one third over bottom of an 8-inch spring-form pan.
2 Continue layering this way; Half of the chocolate ice cream, ¼ cup of the chocolate syrup, one third of the crumbs, orange sherbet, ¼ cup chocolate syrup, remaining crumbs, remaining chocolate ice cream and remaining syrup. Sprinkle peanut brittle over top.
3 Freeze at least 3 hours, or overnight.
4 When ready to serve, loosen torte around edge with a knife; release spring on pan and carefully lift off side. Slide torte, still on its metal base, onto a serving plate. Cut into wedges with a sharp knife.

Frozen Strawberry Crown

Ladyfingers frame a delectable mold of ice cream layered with strawberry sauce

Makes 8 servings.

2 pints strawberries, washed and hulled
1 cup sugar
8 ladyfingers, split
1 quart vanilla ice cream, slightly softened

1 Set aside 24 whole strawberries for garnish. Mash remaining in a medium-size saucepan; stir

(continued)

in sugar; heat to boiling. Cook, stirring often, 15 minutes; cool completely.

2 Butter a 6-inch spring-form pan. Stand ladyfingers, ¼ inch apart, around edge in pan; lay remaining in bottom. Spoon one third of the ice cream into pan; drizzle with ¼ cup sauce. Make two more layers of each, saving any remaining sauce; freeze.

3 When ready to serve, loosen dessert around edge with knife; remove side of pan. Place dessert, still on metal base, on a serving plate. Garnish with whole strawberries; drizzle with remaining sauce.

Rainbow Ice-Cream Cake

Your freezer does all the work and you take all the bows. This party dessert is an easy make-ahead

Bake at 350° for 30 minutes.
Makes 16 servings.

1 package chocolate cake mix
2 eggs
  Water
1 quart strawberry ice cream, softened
1 quart pistachio ice cream, softened
2 envelopes (1½ ounces each) whipped topping mix
  Milk
  Red food coloring
1 tablespoon light rum (optional)
  Chopped pistachio nuts

1 Grease two 9x1½-inch round layer-cake pans; dust with flour; tap out any excess.

2 Prepare cake mix with eggs and water, following label directions; pour into prepared pans.

3 Bake in moderate oven (350°) 30 minutes, or until centers spring back when lightly pressed with fingertip. Cool in pans on wire racks 10 minutes. Loosen layers around edges with a knife; turn out onto racks; cool completely. Split each layer, using a sawing motion with a sharp knife.

4 While layers bake, cut two 18-inch lengths of plastic wrap and fit into two 8-inch layer-cake pans.

5 Spread half the strawberry ice cream evenly in each cake pan. Top with half the pistachio ice cream in each pan. (Or use your favorite flavor combinations.) Cover ice cream with plastic wrap and freeze until ready to use.

6 Place one split cake layer on cookie sheet.

As pretty as a picture, **Rainbow Ice Cream Cake** is a make-ahead specialty.

Remove one ice-cream layer from pan; peel off transparent wrap and place on split layer; repeat with 2 more split layers and second ice-cream layer. (The extra split layer will make a nice treat for supper topped with a scoop of coffee ice cream.) Freeze entire cake while making frosting.

7 Beat whipped topping mix with milk, following label directions. Tint a pale pink with red food coloring and flavor with rum, if you wish.

8 Frost side and top of cake with part of frosting; pile remaining frosting onto center of cake and swirl out with teaspoon and sprinkle with pistachio nuts.

9 Freeze until frosting is firm; then cover with plastic wrap.

10 When ready to serve, loosen cake around edge of cookie sheet with a spatula dipped in hot water; transfer to serving plate with spatula and pancake turner. Cut with a sharp knife, or try your electric knife.

Royal Baked Alaska

A long-time favorite with a regal look

Bake at 425° for 5 minutes.
Makes 12 servings.

1 package loaf-size pound cake mix
½ gallon brick ice cream

4 egg whites
1 teaspoon vanilla
½ cup sugar

1 Prepare cake mix and bake in a greased cake pan, 9x9x2, following label directions.
2 When ready to put dessert together, place cake layer on 2 double-thick wide strips of foil crisscrossed on a cookie sheet. (This makes handling easier when dessert is hot from the oven.) Remove ice cream from carton and place on top of cake; trim cake to within ½ inch of ice cream. Freeze while making meringue.
3 Beat egg whites with vanilla until foamy-white and double in volume in a large bowl; sprinkle in sugar, a tablespoon at a time, beating all the time until sugar completely dissolves and meringue stands in firm peaks.
4 Spread over ice cream and cake, swirling in peaks, to cover completely. (Work quickly so ice cream doesn't melt.)
5 Bake in hot oven (425°) 5 minutes, or until peaks of meringue are toasty-golden. Slide onto a chilled serving plate; pull out foil strips. Cut dessert in slices with a thin, sharp-blade knife.

Cantaloupe Alaska

This festive baked ice-cream dessert is much easier to make than you might think. If you have a freezer, divide ice cream into 6 mounds and freeze very firm before fixing cantaloupe and beating meringue

Bake at 450° for 2 to 3 minutes.
Makes 6 servings.

4 egg whites
¼ teaspoon cream of tartar
¼ teaspoon salt
¼ cup sugar
1 ripe large cantaloupe
1 quart pistachio ice cream
Chopped pistachio nuts

1 Place egg whites, cream of tartar, and salt in large bowl; beat until foamy; add sugar, 1 tablespoon at a time, beating after each addition until meringue forms stiff peaks.
2 Cut cantaloupe into 6 wedges; scoop out seeds; cut a thin slice from bottom of each wedge to make it stand steady; place on cookie sheet or breadboard; top each wedge with large scoop of very firm ice cream; cover completely with meringue, spreading it down to cantaloupe rind.

3 Bake in very hot oven (450°) 2 to 3 minutes, or until meringue is tipped with gold; sprinkle lightly with pistachio nuts; serve at once.

Rainbow Party Pie

Scoop sherbets into a ladyfinger crust and top with sparkly sauce

Makes 6 to 8 servings.

12 ladyfingers
¼ cup apricot preserves
1 pint lime sherbet
1 pint orange sherbet
1 pint lemon sherbet
LEMON SPARKLE SAUCE (recipe follows)

1 Separate ladyfingers to make 24 pieces; spread flat side of each with preserves. Stand upright, rounded side out, ½ inch apart, around edge of a 9-inch pie plate; lay remaining in bottom.
2 Scoop sherbets into small balls; pile into prepared crust. Freeze at least four hours, or overnight.
3 When ready to serve, drizzle with part of the LEMON SPARKLE SAUCE; cut pie into wedges. Pass remaining sauce separately.

LEMON SPARKLE SAUCE
Mix ½ cup sugar and 1 tablespoon cornstarch in a small saucepan; stir in 1 cup water. Cook, stirring constantly, until mixture thickens and bubbles 1 minute; remove from heat. Stir in 3 tablespoons butter or margarine, 3 tablespoons lemon juice and ½ teaspoon grated lemon peel; cool. Makes about 1½ cups.

Coffee Meringue Glacé

Crisp coffee meringue shell is filled with vanilla ice cream, topped with a mocha sauce

Bake at 275° for 1½ to 2 hours.
Makes 10 servings.

4 egg whites
1 cup sugar
3 tablespoons instant coffee powder
⅛ teaspoon salt
1 quart vanilla ice cream
MOCHA SAUCE (recipe, see index)
2 tablespoons finely chopped walnuts

(continued)

1 Beat egg whites until stiff but not dry. Mix sugar with coffee and salt; gradually beat into egg whites, a tablespoon at a time, until meringue stands in firm peaks.
2 Cover cookie sheet with aluminum foil; mark off a 9-inch circle on foil. Spread meringue within circle, building up the edge to about 2 inches.
3 Bake in slow oven (275°) 1½ to 2 hours, or until crisp and dry. Remove from oven; cool. Carefully peel away foil; place meringue on serving plate.
4 Fill shell with ice cream; drizzle with the MOCHA SAUCE. Sprinkle with chopped walnuts. Cut in wedges to serve; spoon more sauce over each serving.

Chocolate Ice Cream Supreme

Made with two kinds of chocolate, a delight for chocolate-lovers

Makes about 2 quarts.

1 cup milk
¼ cup dry cocoa (not a mix)
3 cups cream for whipping
¼ cup finely chopped sweet cooking chocolate
6 egg yolks
1 cup sugar

1 Gradually add milk to cocoa in a medium-size saucepan; mixing until well blended; add cream; heat slowly just until bubbles appear around edge. Stir in chocolate until melted.
2 Beat egg yolks until frothy in small bowl of mixer; gradually add sugar, beating until fluffy-thick. Stir a small portion of hot mixture into egg yolks; add to hot mixture in saucepan. Cook, stirring constantly, over low heat until mixture thickens slightly and coats a spoon. Strain into an 8-cup can of an electric or hand-crank ice cream freezer. Chill until ready to freeze.
3 Freeze, following manufacturer's directions.
4 Unsnap cranking gear, carefully wipe cover and around side of can with a damp cloth; remove dasher. Spoon ice cream into serving dishes. If you prefer ice cream hard-frozen, repack following manufacturer's directions and let stand about 2 hours.

Old-Fashioned Vanilla Ice Cream

Rich with egg yolks and cream

Makes about 2½ quarts.

6 egg yolks
1⅓ cups sugar
½ teaspoon salt
4 cups milk, scalded
2 cups cream for whipping
2 tablespoons vanilla

1 Beat egg yolks with sugar and salt in a medium-size saucepan; stir in 2 cups of the milk. Heat slowly, stirring constantly, *just* until sugar dissolves. Pour into a large bowl; chill until mixture is cold.
2 Stir in remaining milk, cream and vanilla. Pour into 16-cup can of an electric or hand-crank ice cream freezer. Freeze, following manufacturer's directions.
3 Unsnap cranking gear; carefully wipe cover and around side of can with a damp cloth. Lift off lid; remove dasher. Serve immediately. Or, to hard-freeze, repack following manufacturer's directions; let stand two hours. To store in your freezer, lift can from pail and wipe outside to remove all ice and salt; cover. Place in freezer until serving time.

Milk-Chocolate Mousse

Each luscious spoonful just coaxes you into having more. As a party dessert it's a perfect make-ahead choice

Makes 8 servings

1 package (6 ounces) semisweet-chocolate pieces
⅓ cup water
½ cup sugar
⅛ teaspoon salt
2 eggs, separated
1 teaspoon vanilla
2 cups cream for whipping
CANDIED ORANGE SLICES (recipe follows)

1 Combine chocolate pieces and water in a small saucepan; heat very slowly, stirring constantly, until chocolate melts and mixture is smooth. Stir in ¼ cup of the sugar and salt; heat, stirring constantly, until sugar dissolves; remove from heat.
2 Beat egg yolks slightly in a small bowl; very

Chocolate, a meringue, and candied orange slices make **Milk-Chocolate Mousse** a dessert that you'll remember with pleasure.

slowly beat in hot chocolate mixture and vanilla; cool.

3 Beat egg whites until foamy-white and double in volume in a medium-size bowl; beat in remaining ¼ cup sugar, 1 tablespoon at a time, until meringue stands in firm peaks. Beat cream until stiff in a second medium-size bowl.

4 Fold cooled chocolate mixture into meringue, then fold in whipped cream until no streaks of white remain. Pour into an 8-inch springform pan; cover.

5 Freeze six hours, or until firm.

6 When ready to serve, loosen dessert around edge with a knife; release spring and carefully lift off side of pan. Place dessert, still on its metal base, on a serving plate. Garnish top and side with CANDIED ORANGE SLICES. Cut in wedges.

CANDIED ORANGE SLICES

Cut a small seedless orange into 12 thin slices; halve each. Sprinkle ½ cup sugar on a large plate; place orange slices in a single layer on top. Let stand at room temperature, turning two or three times, 2 hours, or until glazed. Remove and place on wax paper to dry slightly.

Raspberry Mousse

Serve with ladyfingers for an elegant finale

Makes 6 to 8 servings.

2 packages frozen red raspberries, thawed
1 cup cream for whipping

⅔ cup 10X (confectioners' powdered) sugar
⅛ teaspoon salt
¼ cup cream, whipped (for topping)

1 Save 3 raspberries for garnish; press remaining through sieve into medium-size bowl.

2 Beat 1 cup cream until foamy in second bowl; add sugar and salt; beat until stiff; gently fold into sieved raspberries; spoon into dry ice-cube tray.

3 Freeze until ice crystals form around edge; stir until smooth; spoon into a 4-cup fancy mold or bowl; freeze until firm.

4 To unmold; Loosen around edge with small spatula; dip mold or bowl *very quickly* into hot water; set serving plate on top; turn upside down; lift off mold; garnish with whipped cream and raspberries.

Maple Butter-Nut Charlotte

Crispy sugar wafers frame a delectably rich mousselike cream

Makes 8 to 12 servings.

1¼ cups butter-blended syrup
3 egg whites
2 cups cream for whipping
2 teaspoons vanilla
¾ cup chopped walnuts
1 package (3 ounces) sugar wafers

1 Heat syrup to boiling in medium-size saucepan; boil 3 minutes.

(continued)

2 Beat egg whites until they stand in firm peaks in medium-size bowl. Beating constantly, *gradually* pour in hot syrup in a thin stream; continue beating about 5 minutes, or until syrup mixture is cool. (Mixture will be liquid, not fluffy like meringue.)

3 Beat 1½ cups cream and vanilla until stiff in large bowl. (Save remaining cream for Step 5.) Gradually fold in cooled syrup mixture, then walnuts.

4 Stand sugar wafers, about ½ inch apart, around side of a 7-inch spring-form pan; lay remaining wafers on bottom. Spoon in cream mixture; freeze 4 hours, or until firm.

5 Beat saved ½ cup cream until stiff in small bowl; spread over top; decorate with walnut halves, if you wish. Freeze until serving time.

6 Release spring and lift off side of pan; place charlotte on serving plate. Cut into wedge-shape pieces.

Orange Blossom Ice Cream

Top this tangy-sweet frosty with sparkling rivulets of burnt-sugar sauce

Makes 6 to 8 servings.

> 1¼ cups milk
> ⅔ cup sugar
> 1 can (6 ounces) frozen concentrated orange juice
> 1 cup cream for whipping
> ⅛ teaspoon salt
> 1 tablespoon lemon juice
> 1 egg white, stiffly beaten
> BURNT-SUGAR SAUCE *(recipe follows)*

1 Combine milk and sugar in medium-size saucepan; heat, stirring constantly, just until sugar is dissolved. Remove from heat.

2 Stir in frozen orange juice, cream, salt and lemon juice. (Mixture will look curdled, but flecks will disappear when frozen.)

3 Pour into pan, 8x8x2, or 2 ice-cube trays; freeze until firm about 1 inch in from edge. Spoon into chilled large bowl; beat quickly until fluffy-smooth; fold in beaten egg white.

4 Return to pan; freeze 30 minutes; stir again. Freeze 2 to 3 hours longer, or until firm.

An any-time treat, **Orange Blossom Ice Cream** and **Burnt-Sugar Sauce** combine for a flavor-filled fruit dessert.

5 Spoon into sherbet glasses; pour BURNT-SUGAR SAUCE over.

BURNT-SUGAR SAUCE

Heat 1½ cups sugar in medium-size heavy frying pan or saucepan, stirring constantly with a wooden spoon, until melted into a golden syrup; remove from heat. Stir in 1 cup boiling water *very slowly*. (Watch it, as mixture will splatter.) Return to heat; cook, stirring constantly, until sugar mixture is smooth and syrupy. (Sauce will be thin, but will thicken as it cools.) Makes about 2 cups.

Note: Store any left over in a covered jar; reheat by setting jar in a pan of hot water for a few minutes.

Brandied Peach Ice Cream

Top with crushed walnut brittle, if you wish

Makes about 2 quarts.

4 medium-size peaches, peeled, pitted and
*   diced (about 2 cups)*
¼ cup brandy
3 cups cream for whipping
1 cup sugar

1 Toss peaches with brandy in a large bowl; mash slightly.
2 Combine 1 cup of the cream with sugar in a small saucepan; heat slowly, stirring constantly, until sugar dissolves. Pour over peach mixture; stir in remaining 2 cups cream.
3 Pour into 8-cup can of an electric or hand-crank ice-cream freezer; freeze, following manufacturer's directions.
4 Unsnap cranking gear; carefully wipe cover and around side of can with damp cloth. Lift off lid; remove dasher. To hard-freeze ice cream, repack, following manufacturer's directions; let stand about 2 hours. Or, to store in your freezer, lift can from pail and wipe outside to remove all ice and salt; cover. Place in freezer until serving time.

Apple-Cinnamon Ice Cream

Reminiscent of apple pie à la mode

Makes 8 to 10 servings.

2 medium-size tart apples, pared, quartered,
*   cored and chopped (2 cups)*
¼ cup finely chopped seedless raisins
½ cup firmly packed brown sugar
½ teaspoon ground cinnamon
¼ cup water
3 pints vanilla ice cream

1 Combine apples, raisins, brown sugar, cinnamon and water in a medium-size saucepan. Heat, stirring constantly, to boiling; cover. Simmer 20 minutes, or until apples are tender. Cool completely.
2 Soften ice cream slightly; spread in a freezer-proof dish, 9x9x2. Drop cooled apple mixture by spoonfuls on top; draw a knife through mixture to marble. Cover.
3 Freeze several hours until firm.

Biscuit Tortoni

A classic ending to an Italian meal

Makes 6 servings.

2 eggs, separated
½ cup sifted 10X (confectioners' powdered)
*   sugar*
1¼ teaspoon vanilla
½ teaspoon almond extract
1 cup   cream for whipping, whipped
⅓ cup drained and chopped maraschino
*   cherries*
¾ cup crushed macaroons

1 Beat egg yolks until light and fluffy. Add 10X sugar, 1 tablespoon at a time, beating well after each addition. Mix in vanilla and almond extract.
2 Beat egg whites until they stand in stiff peaks; fold into egg-yolk mixture. Fold in whipped cream. Stir in maraschino cherries and all but 3 tablespoonfuls of the macaroon crumbs.
3 Spoon into 4-ounce paper soufflé cups. Top with remaining crushed macaroons.
4 Freeze until firm.

Cranberry Tortoni

A splendid autumn choice

Makes 6 servings.

½ cup evaporated milk
1 tablespoon lemon juice
8 marshmallows, cut up
1 can (8 ounces) pineapple tidbits
1 cup canned whole cranberry sauce
2 tablespoons graham cracker crumbs

(continued)

1 Chill evaporated milk in freezing tray about 20 minutes; pour into chilled bowl; whip until it begins to thicken; add lemon juice; whip until very stiff.
2 Fold in marshmallows, pineapple and juice and cranberry sauce.
3 Return to freezing tray or divide among six 4-ounce aluminum-foil molds or paper soufflé cups; freeze until firm; garnish with graham cracker crumbs.

Frozen Eggnog Cheese Squares

For variety, simply chill dessert until set instead of freezing it

Makes 8 to 12 servings.

  2 cups sugar cookie crumbs
  ¼ cup (½ stick) butter or margarine
1½ cups bottled eggnog
  1 package (3 ounces) whipped topping mix
  3 cartons (4 ounces each) whipped cream cheese

1 Blend cookie crumbs and butter or margarine in a medium-size bowl; press half over bottom of a pan, 9x9x2.
2 Combine eggnog and whipped-topping mix in a small deep bowl; beat, following label directions. Slowly beat in cream cheese until well blended.
3 Pour half into prepared pan; sprinkle with remaining crumb mixture; top with remaining cheese mixture.
4 Freeze 3 hours, or until firm. Cut into squares.

Pineapple Sherbet in Orange Cups

With the taste of three fruits

Makes 6 servings.

2 cups buttermilk
1 can (6 ounces) frozen concentrated pineapple juice, thawed
1 cup sugar
6 small oranges, peeled
6 whole strawberries, washed and hulled

1 Combine buttermilk, pineapple juice and sugar in medium-size bowl; beat until well blended.

2 Pour into ice-cube tray, or pan, 8x8x2; freeze until firm almost to middle.
3 Spoon into chilled medium-size bowl; beat until fluffy-smooth. Return to tray; freeze 2 to 3 hours longer, or until firm.
4 Separate sections of each orange slightly to form a cup; place in dessert dishes. Scoop sherbet into center; garnish each with a fresh strawberry.

"Instant" Peach-Orange Sherbet

A quick-fix dessert or one you enjoy much later

Makes 3 servings.

1 package (10 ounces) frozen sliced peaches
1 tablespoon orange-flavor instant breakfast drink

1 Break apart frozen sliced peaches with a fork. Spoon into electric-blender container. Add orange-flavor instant breakfast drink.
2 Start blender at slow speed, beat about 15 seconds; turn off; stir with rubber spatula; turn to high speed and continue alternate beating and stirring about 3 minutes, or *just* until fruit is the consistency of sherbet.
3 Serve immediately or keep frozen in ice cube tray.

Buttermilk-Lime Sherbet

A particularly healthy dessert, rich in vitamins

Makes 6 servings.

  4 cups buttermilk
  1 cup sugar
1½ cups light corn syrup
1½ teaspoons grated lime peel
1½ teaspoons grated lemon peel
  ½ cup lime juice

1 Combine buttermilk and sugar in a large bowl; stir until sugar is completely dissolved. Blend in corn syrup, lime and lemon peels and lime juice.

2 Pour into 2 dry ice-cube trays; freeze until firm about 1 inch around edges. Stir until smooth; freeze until firm.

Lemon Snow Sherbet

This delicately light dessert is a perfect top-off to a bountiful dinner

Makes 8 cups.

4 cups buttermilk
1 cup sugar
1½ cups light corn syrup
1 tablespoon grated lemon peel
½ cup lemon juice

1 Combine all ingredients in a large bowl; stir until sugar is dissolved.
2 Pour into 2 dry ice-cube trays; freeze until firm about 1 inch around edges; stir until smooth; freeze until firm.

Italian Ice

Light and refreshing

Makes 4 to 6 servings.

3 cups water
¾ cup sugar
1 can (6 ounces) frozen concentrated pineapple-orange juice

1 Simmer water and sugar 5 minutes; stir in and melt frozen concentrated pineapple-orange juice.
2 Freeze in freezer tray until mushy-firm. Serve in small paper cups; squeeze cup from bottom or use a spoon.

Grape Ice

Lemon juice adds zest to the grape flavor

Makes 4 to 6 servings.

2¼ cups water
¼ cup light corn syrup
¾ cup sugar
1 can (6 ounces) frozen concentrated grape juice
1 tablespoon lemon juice

1 Simmer water, light corn syrup and sugar 5 minutes; stir in and melt frozen concentrated grape juice. Stir in lemon juice.
2 Freeze in freezer tray until mushy-firm. Serve in small paper cups; squeeze cup from bottom or use a spoon.

Cranberry Ice

A delightful intermezzo at Thanksgiving dinner

Makes 4 to 6 servings.

2¼ cups cranberry juice cocktail
¼ cup light corn syrup
½ cup sugar
2 tablespoons lemon juice

1 Place all ingredients in a medium-size saucepan and simmer, stirring occasionally, until sugar is dissolved.
2 Freeze in freezer tray until mushy-firm. Serve in small paper cups; squeeze cup from bottom or use a spoon.

Some desserts call out for an elegant table. And **Strawberry Cheese Mold** is one of these. (For recipe see p.55.)

Refrigerated Dessert Splendors

When you are looking for a dessert that shimmers, try any one of the many in these pages. From gelatin-based desserts to sponges, Bavarians, cheesecakes, tortes, parfaits, to chiffons, you'll find dessert recipes you'll enjoy making.

TORTES

Spanische Windtorte (Spanish Wind Cake)

The meringue shell should be made the day before you plan to serve it: bake it on a clear, dry day or it will be difficult to make the meringue crisp; use leftover yolks to make a custard

Bake at 225° for 45 minutes,
then for 30 minutes.
Makes 12 servings.

MERINGUE
7 egg whites
½ teaspoon cream of tartar
1¾ cups sugar
   Unglazed brown wrapping paper
   Large pastry bag
   Number 4 or 5 large star tip
FILLING
2 cups heavy cream
2 tablespoons 10X (confectioners') sugar (optional)
1 tablespoon vanilla
2 packages (10 ounces each) quick-thaw frozen peaches, partially thawed
1 package (10 ounces) frozen raspberries, partially thawed
1 cup frozen blueberries (from a 10-ounce package), thawed

1 Line 2 cooky sheets with brown paper. Draw 2 eight-inch circles 1 inch apart on one, and 1 eight-inch circle on the other, using an 8-inch cake pan as a guide.

2 Beat 3 egg whites with ¼ teaspoon of the cream of tartar until foamy and soft peaks form when beater is slowly raised. Sprinkle in ¾ cup of the sugar *very slowly, about 1 tablespoon every ½ minute,* beating constantly with mixer on high, until sugar dissolves completely and meringue forms firm peaks when beater is lifted.
3 Spoon meringue into pastry bag fitted with a number 4 or 5 star tip. Pipe a ¾-inch circle of meringue just inside one outline. Continue circle in a closed spiral that ends in the center. (This is the base for your windtorte.) Pipe remaining meringue just inside the other two outlines to make 2 rings about ¾-inch wide. If you have meringue left, press a second layer on top of each ring to make a double layer.
4 Bake in very slow oven (225°) for 45 minutes; turn off oven heat and leave meringues in oven with oven door closed for 45 minutes longer. Gently peel off paper; cool.
5 Beat remaining 4 egg whites, remaining ¼ teaspoon cream of tartar and ¾ cup of the remaining sugar as in Step 2. Fold in remaining ¼ cup sugar with rubber scraper.
6 Line cooky sheet with a clean sheet of brown paper. Place the cooled meringue layer on paper; stack the 2 circles on top using a little meringue between each for cement. Frost outside of shell with a thin, smooth layer of meringue. Spoon remaining meringue into pastry bag. Pipe a decorative scalloped border around the top and bottom edge of shell; decorate side with swirls.
7 On a second piece of brown paper, draw a 6-inch circle. Fill in circle with about ¼-inch-thick layer of meringue; pipe a decorative scalloped border on edge; pipe three "S" shapes on paper. Reserve about 1 tablespoon meringue for assembling the lid.
8 Bake in very slow oven (225°) 30 minutes. Turn off oven heat and leave meringues in oven, with oven door closed, overnight. Meringue should then be completely dry. (Should it feel slightly sticky, turn oven heat to low [200°] for about 5 minutes; turn off and leave meringue in oven to dry completely.) Lean the three "S" shapes together on top of lid; attach in center and at base of each with a bit of reserved meringue to form a handle; let dry. Store in a large

(continued)

container with a tight-fitting lid to keep meringue dry and crisp. OR: Carefully place in a plastic bag and store in a dry place. (A gas oven with a pilot light is ideal.) Again, if the meringue feels sticky, place in oven and turn oven to low (200°) for 5 minutes.

9 To fill: Place shell on flat serving plate or tray. Whip the cream with sugar (optional) and vanilla till stiff. Drain fruits and reserve a few perfect ones for top. Layer fruits with cream in shell, drizzling a little peach or raspberry juice over each layer, if you wish; arrange reserved fruits on top. Serve immediately.

10 To serve: Put on the lid to present the dessert. Cut shell with a serrated knife into about 1½- to 2-inch wide pieces; remove each piece to a plate and spoon some of filling over. Don't worry if meringue crumbles.

Note: Ice cream or sherbet balls can be used instead of cream filling, if you wish.

Lemon Angel Torte

Creamiest lemon filling imaginable billows high in a sweet meringue shell

Bake at 275° for 1 hour.
Makes on 9-inch torte.

MERINGUE SHELL
4 egg whites
¼ teaspoon cream of tartar
¼ teaspoon salt
1 cup sugar

FILLING
4 egg yolks
1 whole egg
⅔ cup sugar
1 tablespoon grated lemon rind
¼ cup lemon juice
1 cup cream for whipping

1 Prepare pie plate for meringue shell this way: Fit a 15x2-inch strip of foil into a 9-inch pie plate, leaving a 2-inch overhang on each end. (This makes shell easy to remove to serving plate). Coat pie plate and strip generously with butter or margarine; dust with flour to coat completely; tap out any excess.

2 Make meringue shell: Beat egg whites with cream of tartar and salt until foamy-white and double in volume in large bowl. Beat in sugar, 1 tablespoon at a time, beating well after each, until sugar is completely dissolved and meringue stands in firm peaks. (Beating will take about 25 minutes in all with an electric beater.)

3 Spread meringue into prepared pie plate, dishing center slightly and swirling around edge.

4 Bake in very slow oven (275°) 1 hour, or until delicately golden. Cool completely in pie plate on wire rack.

5 To remove, run a knife around edge, lifting foil strip at the same time, to loosen completely. Lift out with spatula and foil; peel off foil; place shell on serving plate. If made ahead, leave in pie plate until ready to fill.

6 Make filling: Beat egg yolks and whole egg slightly in top of double boiler; stir in sugar, and lemon rind and juice.

7 Cook over simmering water, stirring constantly, 10 minutes, or until thick. Chill until mixture mounds slightly.

8 Beat cream until stiff in small bowl; fold into lemon mixture. Spoon lightly into cooled meringue shell on serving plate. Chill at least 2 hours, or until softly set.

9 Garnish with a slice of lemon dipped in sugar, if you wish. Cut in wedges.

Party Pink Pouf Torte

Meringue base for this luscious sweet ''bakes'' while you sleep, then gets its rosy berry crown an hour before serving time

Makes one 8-inch torte.

6 egg whites
½ teaspoon cream of tartar
¼ teaspoon salt
1½ cups sugar
1 teaspoon vanilla
¼ cup slivered blanched almonds
2 cups (1 pint) strawberries, washed
   OR: 1 package (10 ounces) frozen sliced strawberries, thawed
1 cup cream for whipping
   Red food coloring

1 Turn on oven to hot (400°).

2 Beat egg whites, cream of tartar, and salt until foamy-white and double in volume in large bowl.

3 Beat in sugar, 1 tablespoon at a time, beating well after each, until meringue stands in firm peaks. (Sugar should be completely dissolved before adding more. Beating should take about 30 minutes.) Fold in vanilla.

4 Spoon meringue into buttered 8-inch spring-form pan; make a slight hollow in middle with a spoon; sprinkle slivered almonds over.

5 Place in hot oven (400°); close oven door

(continued)

Some tortes hide their surprises. Not **Party Pink Pouf Torte** which proudly displays its strawberries. **Mocha Bavarian** is other dessert.

and turn heat off immediately. Leave torte to slow-bake, *without peeking even once,* overnight, or at least 12 hours.

6 Remove torte from oven; loosen around edge with knife; release spring and carefully lift off side of pan. Carefully slide torte off pan onto serving plate.

7 About 1 hour before serving, hull and slice enough strawberries to make 1 cup; spoon over meringue. (If using frozen berries, drain, saving a few for garnish.)

8 Beat cream until stiff in small bowl; blend in a few drops red food coloring to tint a delicate pink. Spoon over strawberries; top with a halved berry; chill. Garnish torte with remaining whole or sliced berries; slice in wedges with a sharp knife.

Raspberry Angel Torte

Multi-layered, with an abundance of filling

Bake at 300° for 30 minutes.
Makes 8 servings.

6 egg whites
¼ teaspoon cream of tartar
1½ cups sugar
1 cup flaked coconut
½ cup cornstarch
RASPBERRY FILLING *(recipe follows)*
1 container (9 ounces) frozen whipped topping, thawed

1 Grease 3 large cookie sheets; dust with flour, tapping off any excess. Draw 2 circles, each

Cut into **Raspberry Angel Torte** and you'll not regret the time it took you to put it together.

6½ inches, on each of the cookie sheets, using a salad plate as a guide. (If you do not have enough cookie sheets or oven space to bake six layers at once, shape meringue on greased floured foil and let stand at room temperature until first batch is baked. Then simply slide foil onto cookie sheets.)

2 Beat egg whites with cream of tartar until foamy-white in a large bowl. Sprinkle in sugar, 1 tablespoon at a time, beating all the time until sugar dissolves completely and meringue stands in firm peaks. (Beating will take about 30 minutes in all with an electric beater.)

3 Mix coconut and cornstarch in a small bowl; fold into meringue until blended. Spoon meringue, dividing evenly, into the 6 circles on cookie sheets; spread to edges. (Or fit a large star tip onto a pastry bag; spoon meringue into bag; press out into circles.)

4 Bake in slow oven (300°) 30 minutes, or until firm and lightly golden. Cool 5 minutes on cookie sheets on wire racks; loosen layers carefully with a spatula; slide onto racks. Cool layers completely.

5 Make RASPBERRY FILLING. Place one meringue layer on a large serving plate; spread with a thin layer of whipped topping, then spoon about one fifth of the raspberry mixture over top. Repeat filling and stacking with four more layers; top with plain layer. Chill several hours to mellow and soften meringue. Just before serving, spoon remaining whipped topping in center; garnish with raspberries, if you wish. Cut torte in wedges with a sharp knife and a sawing motion.

RASPBERRY FILLING

Thaw 2 packages (10 ounces each) frozen red raspberries, following label directions. Drain syrup into a 2-cup measure; stir in ½ cup water. Mix 3 tablespoons cornstarch and 2 tablespoons sugar in a medium-size saucepan; stir in syrup mixture. Cook, stirring constantly, until mixture thickens and bubbles 1 minute; cool. Fold in raspberries. (To make garnish: After thawing berries, pick out 6 of the largest, stand on a plate, and return to freezer until just before serving time.)

Strawberry Chantilly Torte

So rich! Tiers of cake and almond meringue are filled and crowned with whipped cream and rosy fruit

Bake at 350° for 30 minutes.
Makes 8 to 10 servings.

1 cup sifted cake flour
1 teaspoon baking powder
¼ teaspoon salt
½ cup (1 stick) butter or margarine
1½ cups sugar
5 eggs, separated
1 teaspoon vanilla
3 tablespoons milk
¾ teaspoon almond extract
½ cup toasted slivered almonds (from a 5-ounce can)
2 pints strawberries
2 cups cream for whipping

1 Butter bottoms of two 9x1½-inch layer-cake pans; dust lightly with flour, tapping out any excess.

2 Sift flour, baking powder, and salt onto wax paper.

3 Cream butter or margarine with ½ cup of the sugar until fluffy in a medium-size bowl; beat in egg yolks, one at a time, until blended, then beat in vanilla and milk.

4 Fold in flour mixture until blended; spread evenly in prepared pans.

5 Beat egg whites with ¼ teaspoon of the almond extract until foamy-white and double in volume in a large bowl; sprinkle in ¾ cup of the remaining sugar, 1 tablespoon at a time, beating all the time until sugar dissolves completely and meringue stands in firm peaks. Spread evenly over batter in pans; sprinkle with almonds.

6 Bake in moderate oven (350°) 30 minutes, or until meringue is delicately browned.

7 Cool layers in pans on wire racks 5 minutes; loosen around edges with a knife; turn each out onto palm of hand, then place, meringue side up, on racks; cool completely.

8 Wash strawberries, hull, and quarter.

9 Beat cream with remaining ¼ cup sugar and

(continued)

With its alternate layers of butter cake and crispy almond meringue, **Strawberry Chantilly Torte** will be regarded as one of your gourmet recipes.

½ teaspoon almond extract until stiff in a medium-size bowl.

10 Place 1 cake layer on a large serving plate; top with about half of the whipped cream and strawberries. Repeat with second cake layer and remaining strawberries and whipped cream. Cut cake into wedges with a sharp knife.

CHEESECAKES

Chocolate Ripple Cheesecake

Rivulets of bitter chocolate twirl through its cream-rich filling

Bake at 400° for 10 minutes,
then at 325° for 1 hour.
Makes 12 servings.

CRUST
¼ cup (½ stick) butter or margarine
¼ cup granulated sugar
¼ cup firmly packed brown sugar
¾ cup sifted all-purpose flour
¼ teaspoon baking powder
Dash of salt

CAKE
1 square unsweetened chocolate
3 packages (8 ounces each) cream cheese
1¼ cups granulated sugar
6 eggs, separated
6 tablespoons all-purpose flour
1 teaspoon grated lemon rind
2 tablespoons lemon juice
1 teaspoon vanilla
1 cup cream for whipping

1 Make crust: Cream butter or margarine with granulated and brown sugars until fluffy in small bowl; gradually sift in flour, baking powder, and salt, blending well. Press evenly into bottom of 9-inch spring-form pan.
2 Bake in hot oven (400°) 10 minutes, or until lightly golden; remove from oven. (Leave heat on.) Cool in pan on wire rack while making cake.
3 Make cake: Melt chocolate in cup over simmering water; set aside but keep melted for Step 7.
4 Soften cream cheese in large bowl; gradually beat in sugar until fluffy. Beat in egg yolks just

until blended; stir in flour, lemon rind and juice, and vanilla.
5 Beat egg whites until they form soft peaks in medium-size bowl. Beat cream until stiff in small bowl.
6 Fold beaten egg whites, then cream, into egg-yolk mixture until no streaks of white or yellow remain.
7 Spoon about a third on cooled crust; drizzle about a teaspoonful of melted chocolate over; repeat 2 more times, ending with chocolate. Cut through mixture with a long thin knife to swirl chocolate.
8 Place pan in oven; reduce heat to slow (325°); bake 1 hour. Turn heat off and let cake remain in oven *with door closed* 1 hour longer.
9 Remove cake from oven; cool in pan on wire rack at least 2 hours. To serve, loosen cake around edge with knife; release spring and carefully lift off side of pan; place cake, still on its metal base from spring-form pan, on serving plate. Cut in wedges.

Lemon Cheesecake

Your refrigerator "bakes" this shimmery-top gem of creamy cottage cheese and tangy gelatin

Makes 8 servings.

1 package (6 ounces) lemon-flavor gelatin
2 cups hot water
½ cup cold water
2 eggs, separated
3 cups (1½ pounds) cream-style cottage cheese
1 teaspoon grated lemon rind
Dash of salt
¼ cup sugar
1 cup cream for whipping
Fresh mint

1 Dissolve gelatin in hot water in a medium-size saucepan. Pour ½ cup into a 1-cup measure; stir in cold water; set aside at room temperature for Step 3 while preparing custard mixture.
2 Beat egg yolks slightly in a small bowl; slowly stir in a generous ½ cup of the hot gelatin mixture, then stir back into remaining gelatin mixture in saucepan. Cook, stirring constantly, 3 minutes; remove from heat. Chill 30 minutes, or just until as thick as unbeaten egg white.
3 Pour the saved 1 cup gelatin mixture into an 8-cup mold; chill 15 minutes, or just until sticky-firm.

(continued)

4 Press cottage cheese through a sieve into a large bowl; stir in thickened gelatin-custard mixture, lemon rind, and salt.

5 Beat egg whites until foamy-white and double in volume in a small bowl; beat in sugar, 1 tablespoon at a time, until meringue forms soft peaks. Beat cream until stiff in a medium-size bowl.

6 Fold meringue, then whipped cream into thickened gelatin-cheese mixture until no streaks of white remain; spoon over *sticky-firm layer* in mold. Chill at least 6 hours, or until firm.

7 When ready to serve, run a sharp-tip thin-blade knife around top of dessert, then dip mold *very quickly* in and out of a pan of hot water. Cover with a serving plate; turn upside down; gently lift off mold. Garnish with sprigs of fresh mint.

Royal Cheddar Cheesecake

Mild yellow and cream cheeses blend for the richest filling imaginable

Bake at 500° for 12 minutes,
then at 250° for 2 hours.
Makes 12 servings.

1½ cups zwieback crumbs (about 18 slices)
3 tablespoons sugar (for crust)
2 teaspoons grated lemon rind
6 tablespoons (¾ stick) butter or margarine, melted
4 packages (8 ounces each) cream cheese
1 cup finely grated mild Cheddar cheese
1¾ cups sugar (for filling)
5 eggs
½ cup cream for whipping
½ teaspoon vanilla

1 Mix zwieback crumbs with the 3 tablespoons sugar and 1 teaspoon of the grated lemon rind in a small bowl; blend in melted butter or margarine. Press evenly over bottom and up side of a buttered 8-inch spring-form pan. Set pan on a 12-inch-long piece of double-thick foil; fold foil up around side to catch any butter mixture that may bubble out as cake bakes. Chill while making filling.

2 Soften cream cheese in a large bowl; slowly beat in Cheddar cheese until no flecks of yellow remain. Beat in 1¾ cups sugar until creamy-smooth.

3 Beat in eggs, one at a time; stir in cream, vanilla, and remaining 1 teaspoon lemon rind. Pour into prepared crust.

4 Bake in extremely hot oven (500°) 12 minutes; lower heat to very slow (250°). Continue baking 2 hours, or until firm on top.

5 Cool cake completely in pan on a wire rack, then remove foil wrapping. Loosen cake around edge with a knife; release spring and carefully lift off side of pan, leaving cake on its metal base. Garnish with fresh fruit of your choice, if you wish.

You can use Cheddar in a cheesecake as the golden **Royal Cheddar Cheesecake** richly proves.

Family Circle's Best Cheesecake

This is our favorite: one bite, and it will become one of yours

Bake at 475° for 10 minutes,
then at 200° for 1 hour.
Makes 16 servings.

1 cup graham-cracker crumbs (from a 13½-ounce package)
1 tablespoon sugar (for crust)
½ teaspoon ground cinnamon
1 tablespoon butter or margarine, melted (for crust)
5 packages (8 ounces each) cream cheese
1¾ cups sugar (for cake)
3 tablespoons all-purpose flour
1½ teaspoons grated orange rind
5 eggs
2 egg yolks
¼ cup milk
ORANGE GLAZE (recipe follows)

1 Combine graham-cracker crumbs, 1 tablespoon sugar and cinnamon in a small bowl; blend in the melted butter or margarine. Press firmly over bottom of a lightly greased 9-inch spring-form pan. Chill briefly before filling.
2 Let cream cheese soften in a large bowl; blend in sugar, flour and orange rind. Beat with electric mixer until light and fluffy. Add eggs and egg yolks, one at a time, beating well after each addition; stir in milk; pour into crumb crust.
3 Bake in hot oven (475°) 10 minutes; lower temperature to 200° and bake 1 hour longer; let cake remain in oven until cool (about 1 hour).
4 Remove from oven; cool completely on a wire rack; loosen around edge with a knife; release spring and remove side of pan. Top with ORANGE GLAZE.

ORANGE GLAZE
Drain the syrup from a 10 ounce jar mandarin oranges; reserve ½ cup syrup. Combine 2 teaspoons cornstarch and 1 teaspoon sugar in a small saucepan. Slowly stir in reserved syrup; cook, stirring constantly, over medium heat, until mixture thickens and bubbles 1 minute; cool. Dip the orange slices in glaze before placing them on the cake.

BAVARIANS

When looking for a quick-fix dessert, try **Bavarian Royale.** You'll be delighted at the rich flavor.

Bavarian Royale

Creamy, delicious coffee Bavarian cream combined with fluffy sponge cake is the perfect show-off dessert

Makes 12 servings.

2 envelopes unflavored gelatin
1 cup sugar
6 eggs, separated
1 tablespoon instant coffee powder
¼ teaspoon ground cinnamon
Dash of salt
3 cups milk
1 packaged jelly roll (about 8 ounces)

1 Combine gelatin and ½ cup of the sugar in a medium-size saucepan. Add the egg yolks, instant coffee, cinnamon, salt and milk. Beat with a wire whip or rotary beater until smooth.
2 Cook, stirring constantly, over low heat, until mixture thickens slightly and coats spoon. Pour immediately into a large bowl. Place bowl in pan partly filled with ice and water to speed setting. Chill, stirring often, until as thick as unbeaten egg white.
3 Beat egg whites until foamy-white and double in volume in a medium-size bowl. Beat in the remaining ½ cup sugar, 1 tablespoon at a time, until meringue stands in soft peaks. Fold into chilled gelatin mixture.
4 Pour half the gelatin mixture into an 8-cup glass bowl. Chill, while keeping the remaining gelatin mixture at room temperature.
5 Cut jelly roll into ½-inch-thick slices. Arrange over gelatin in glass bowl, pressing slices against sides.

(continued)

6 Spoon the remaining gelatin mixture around slices and into center. Chill at least 3 hours. Garnish with mounds of whipped cream or dessert topping and strawberries, if you wish.

Apricot Bavarian

For a pleasant flavor-blend, serve with crisp cookies

Makes 8 servings.

1 cup dried apricots (from an 11-ounce package)
Water
¾ cup sugar
1 envelope unflavored gelatin
⅛ teaspoon salt
2 eggs, separated
1½ cups cream for whipping

1 Combine apricots and 1¼ cups water in a small saucepan. Heat to boiling, then simmer 15 minutes; drain liquid into a small bowl.
2 Press apricots through a sieve into a small bowl; measure, then add enough of the apricot liquid to make 1 cup. Add water to remaining apricot liquid to make ¾ cup.
3 Mix ½ cup of the sugar, gelatin, and salt in a medium-size saucepan; beat in the ¾ cup apricot liquid and egg yolks. Cook over low heat, stirring constantly, until gelatin dissolves and mixture thickens slightly; stir in the 1 cup puréed apricot mixture. Pour into a medium-size bowl.
4 Place bowl in a pan of ice and water to speed setting. Chill, stirring often, just until as thick as unbeaten egg white.
5 While apricot mixture chills, beat egg whites until foamy-white in a small bowl; beat in remaining ¼ cup sugar until meringue stands in firm peaks. Beat cream until stiff in a medium-size bowl. Fold meringue, then whipped cream into thickened gelatin mixture until no streaks of white remain; spoon into a 6-cup mold. Chill several hours, or until firm.
6 When ready to serve, loosen dessert around edge with a knife; dip mold *very quickly* in and out of hot water. Cover with a serving plate; turn upside down; gently lift off mold. Garnish with mint and clusters of dried apricot halves folded around maraschino cherries, if you wish.

Mocha Bavarian

A lighter version of the classic recipe

Makes 8 servings.

5 teaspoons freeze-dried instant coffee
Cold water
⅔ cup sugar
⅓ cup dry cocoa (not a mix)
2 envelopes unflavored gelatin
⅛ teaspoon salt
2 cups milk
1 teaspoon vanilla
1 container (9 ounces) frozen whipped topping, thawed
¾ teaspoon rum flavoring or extract

1 Dissolve 4 teaspoons of the coffee in 1½ cups water in a 2-cup measure or bowl.
2 Mix sugar, cocoa, gelatin, and salt in a medium-size saucepan; stir in milk. Heat slowly, stirring constantly, until gelatin dissolves; stir in the 1½ cups coffee and vanilla. Pour into a large bowl.
3 Place bowl in a pan of ice and water to speed setting. Chill, stirring several times, just until as thick as unbeaten egg white. Fold in half of the whipped topping until no streaks of white remain; spoon into a 6-cup mold. Chill several hours, or until firm.
4 When ready to serve, loosen dessert around edge with a knife; dip mold *very quickly* in and out of hot water. Cover with a serving plate; turn upside down; gently lift off mold.
5 Dissolve remaining 1 teaspoon coffee in 3 tablespoons water in a cup; stir in rum flavoring. Fold into remaining whipped topping. Spoon over dessert; sprinkle lightly with grated unsweetened or semisweet chocolate, if you wish.

Chocolate Velvet Bavarian

One mouthful will prove it lives up to its name

Makes 6 to 8 servings.

1 envelope unflavored gelatin
¾ cup sugar
½ teaspoon salt
¼ teaspoon nutmeg
3 squares unsweetened chocolate
1 cup milk
½ cup cold brewed coffee
1 teaspoon vanilla

4 eggs, separated
1 cup cream for whipping

1 Mix gelatin, ½ cup of the sugar, salt, and nutmeg in top of a double boiler; add chocolate, milk, coffee, and vanilla. (Save remaining ¼ cup sugar for Step 3.) Heat, stirring constantly, over simmering water until chocolate melts, then beat until smooth.
2 Beat egg yolks in a medium-size bowl; stir in about ½ cup of the hot chocolate mixture; stir back into remaining in top of double boiler. Cook, stirring constantly, over simmering water 3 to 5 minutes, or until mixture thickens and coats a metal spoon; remove from heat. Strain into a large bowl; chill just until as thick as unbeaten egg white.
3 Beat egg whites until foamy-white and double in volume in a medium-size bowl; beat in saved ¼ cup sugar, a tablespoon at a time, until meringue forms soft peaks. Beat cream until stiff in a second bowl. Beat chilled chocolate-gelatin mixture until fluffy; fold in meringue, then whipped cream.
4 Pour into a 6-cup mold; chill several hours, overnight, or until firm.
5 Unmold onto serving plate. Garnish with peppermint patties, if you wish.

Raspberry Chiffon Charlotte

Golden pound-cake strips circle a delectably rich cloudlike raspberry mold

Makes 8 servings.

3 eggs, separated
½ cup water
1 package (3 ounces) raspberry-flavor gelatin
⅛ teaspoon salt
1 package (10 ounces) frozen red raspberries
1 tablespoon lemon juice
9 slices pound cake, cut ⅜ inch thick (from a 12-ounce frozen pound cake)
¾ cup sugar

1 Beat egg yolks with water in top of double boiler. (Save egg whites for Step 4.) Stir in gelatin, salt, and half of the frozen raspberries. Cook, stirring constantly, over simmering water until raspberries thaw and gelatin dissolves. Remove from heat.
2 Stir in remaining raspberries and lemon juice until raspberries thaw; press through a sieve into a large bowl to remove raspberry seeds.

(continued)

Some desserts look as though an architect put them together. **Raspberry Chiffon Charlotte** is one of these. But you'll discover how easy it is.

Chill, stirring often, until mixture is as thick as unbeaten egg white.

3 While gelatin mixture chills, trim brown crust off pound cake, then cut each slice into 3 strips. Stand diagonally, about ½ inch apart, around side of a generously buttered 7-inch spring-form pan; lay remaining on bottom.

4 Beat egg whites until foamy-white and double in volume in medium-size bowl; sprinkle in sugar, 1 tablespoon at a time, beating all the time until sugar completely dissolves and meringue stands in firm peaks. Beat chilled gelatin mixture until fluffy.

5 Place bowl of gelatin in a larger bowl or pan partly filled with ice cubes to speed setting; fold in meringue. Continue folding, keeping bowl over ice, until no streaks of white remain and mixture mounds lightly on a spoon.

6 Spoon into prepared pan, making deep swirls on top with spoon. Chill several hours, or until firm.

7 When ready to serve, loosen mold around edge with knife; release spring and carefully lift off side of pan. Place dessert, still on its metal base, on serving plate. Garnish with a ring of frozen whole raspberries, if you wish. Cut mold into wedges.

Note—To make this fresh-fruit garnish, you'll need a second package of frozen raspberries. Thaw just enough so you can pick out the choicest whole ones. Stand them, not touching, in a shallow pan; refreeze until serving time. They'll look and taste just like fresh berries. Use any remaining frozen berries for fruit cup or topping for plain cake squares.

GELATINS

Strawberry Mousse

Served in a soufflé dish, this mousse is an elegant, yet simple, way to savor the season's bounty of luscious red berries

Makes 8 servings.

2 pints (4 cups) strawberries
  OR: 1 package (1 pound) frozen unsugared strawberries, thawed
1 envelope unflavored gelatin
½ cup sugar
½ cup water
2 egg whites

Pinch cream of tartar
1 cup heavy cream

1 Prepare a collar for a 5-cup soufflé dish: Measure off wax paper long enough to encircle dish. Fold in half lengthwise (wax paper should be about 2 inches higher than rim of dish). Fasten collar with tape or string.

2 Wash, hull and pat strawberries dry on paper toweling. Puree berries, a cup at a time, in container of blender. Pour into bowl. Repeat until all are pureed.

3 Combine gelatin and ¼ cup of the sugar in a small saucepan; stir in water. Place over very low heat and stir constantly until gelatin and sugar are dissolved. Cool mixture.

4 Stir cooled gelatin mixture into pureed strawberries. Put bowl in pan partly filled with ice and water to speed setting.

5 Beat egg whites with cream of tartar in small bowl with electric mixer until foamy white. Beat in the remaining ¼ cup sugar, a tablespoon at a time, until meringue stands in soft peaks. Beat cream in another small bowl until soft peaks form.

6 Fold meringue and whipped cream into strawberry mixture until no streaks of white remain. Pour into prepared dish. Refrigerate 4 hours or until set. Remove collar gently, freeing soufflé from wax paper, if necessary, with a small knife. Garnish with additional whipped cream and strawberries, if you wish.

Strawberries on-the-Half-Shell

These strawberry tarts have a new shape, but the same delicious old flavor

Makes 8 servings.

8 baked SWEET PASTRY TART SHELLS *(recipe follows)*
3 ounces cream cheese, softened
3 tablespoons cream or milk
2 to 3 teaspoons honey
½ cup red currant jelly
2 pints strawberries

1 Combine cream cheese, cream and honey in small bowl; beat until smooth. Melt jelly in small saucepan.

2 Just before serving, arrange tart shells on serving plates; spoon a little cheese filling into each. Arrange strawberries on top, cutting berries in half if they are large. Brush with melted jelly. To match picture: Arrange a second unfilled shell over each tart, if you wish.

Make the most of strawberries with **Strawberry Mousse** and **Strawberries-on-the-Half-Shell.**

Sweet Pastry Tart Shells

Bake at 400° for 10 minutes.
Makes about twenty 2½-inch shells.

2¼ cups sifted all-purpose flour
¼ cup sugar
1 cup (2 sticks) butter or margarine
1 egg
1 teaspoon vanilla

1 Mix flour and sugar in large bowl; cut in butter with pastry blender until mixture is crumbly. Add egg and vanilla; mix with a fork just until pastry holds together. Turn out onto lightly floured surface; knead a few times; chill 1 hour or until ready to use.

2 Roll pastry, half at a time, on floured surface to ⅛-inch thickness; cut into 3½- to 4-inch rounds. Mold each round on the outside of 3-inch scallop shells (available in department and cookware stores), or press against outside of fluted tart pans or small aluminum foil muffin pans or 5-ounce custard cups, pinching edge of pastry into pleats to fit snugly.

3 Bake shells on large cookie sheet in hot oven (400°) for 10 minutes or until golden brown. Cool slightly on wire racks; carefully ease pastry from shells or pans. Cool completely on wire racks. Store in tightly covered container in cool place.

Note: Baked shells are fragile. Do not stack more than 2 to 3 high or crowd in container.

Peach Melba

Frozen peaches go into the yummy mold to be topped with sparkly raspberry sauce

Makes 8 servings.

2 packages (10 ounces each) frozen sliced peaches, thawed
6 eggs, separated
2 envelopes unflavored gelatin
1 teaspoon lemon extract
½ cup sugar
1 cup cream for whipping
    MELBA SAUCE (recipe follows)

1 Drain syrup from peaches into a cup. Place fruit in an electric-blender container; cover. Beat until smooth. (If you do not have a blender, chop peaches finely.)
2 Beat egg yolks slightly in the top of a double boiler; stir in peach syrup; sprinkle gelatin over top; let stand several minutes to soften gelatin.
3 Cook, stirring constantly, over simmering water 10 minutes, or until gelatin dissolves and mixture coats a spoon; remove from heat. Stir in peach purée and lemon extract. Pour into a large bowl.
4 Place bowl in a pan of ice and water to speed setting. Chill, stirring often, just until as thick as unbeaten egg white.
5 While gelatin mixture chills, beat egg whites until foamy-white and double in volume in a medium-size bowl; beat in sugar, 1 tablespoon at a time, until sugar dissolves completely and meringue stands in firm peaks. Beat cream until stiff in a medium-size bowl.
6 Fold meringue, then whipped cream into thickened gelatin mixture until no streaks of white remain. Pour into an 8-cup mold. Chill 6 hours, or until firm. (Overnight is even better.)
7 When ready to unmold, run a sharp-tip thin-blade knife around top of dessert, then dip mold very quickly in and out of a pan of hot water. Cover with a serving plate; turn upside down; gently lift off mold. Top with MELBA SAUCE.

MELBA SAUCE
Thaw 1 package (10 ounces) frozen red raspberries; drain syrup into a cup. Mix 1 tablespoon sugar and 2 teaspoons cornstarch in a small saucepan; stir in raspberry syrup. Cook, stirring constantly, until sauce thickens and bubbles 1 minute; fold in raspberries; cool. Makes about 1¼ cups.

Rosé Ring

Without the cream center, you could serve this with an entrée

Makes 8 servings.

2 envelopes unflavored gelatin
¾ cup sugar
¼ teaspoon salt
1 cup water
2½ cups rosé wine
2 tablespoons lemon juice
1 cup cream for whipping
    FROSTED GRAPES (recipe follows)
    Mint

1 Mix gelatin, sugar, and salt in a medium-size saucepan; stir in water. Heat slowly, stirring constantly, until gelatin dissolves; remove from heat. Stir in wine and lemon juice.
2 Pour into a 4-cup tube mold. Chill several hours, or until firm.
3 Just before serving, beat cream until stiff in a medium-size bowl.
4 Loosen dessert around edge and tube with a knife; dip mold very quickly in and out of hot water. Cover with a serving plate; turn upside down; gently lift off mold. Spoon cream into center; place FROSTED GRAPES and mint around edge.

FROSTED GRAPES
Beat 1 egg white slightly with ½ teaspoon water in a small bowl; place 2 to 3 tablespoons granulated sugar in a small dish. Dip small bunches of seedless green grapes into egg white mixture, then into sugar, turning to coat grapes well. Place on paper toweling until dry.

Rice Mold Imperial

Imagine the creamiest of rice puddings turned out as a handsome mold!

Makes 8 to 10 servings.

1 envelope unflavored gelatin
¼ cup water
4 egg yolks
6 tablespoons sugar
3 cups milk
2 teaspoons vanilla
1 cup uncooked regular rice
1 tablespoon grated orange rind
⅛ teaspoon salt
1 jar (8 ounces) candied red cherries

2 tablespoons orange juice
1 cup cream for whipping
¼ cup toasted slivered almonds (from a 5-ounce can)

1 Soften gelatin in water in a cup; set aside for next step.
2 Beat egg yolks slightly in top of a large double boiler; beat in sugar and 1½ cups of the milk. Cook, stirring constantly, over simmering water 15 minutes, or until custard thickens and coats a metal spoon. Stir in softened gelatin until dissolved.
3 Pour into a large bowl; stir in 1 teaspoon of the vanilla. Set aside while cooking rice.
4 Combine rice with water to cover in top of same double boiler. Heat to boiling over direct heat; drain, then return rice to pan. Stir in remaining 1½ cups milk and 1 teaspoon vanilla, orange rind, and salt.
5 Cook, stirring often, over simmering water 40 minutes, or until rice is tender and liquid is absorbed. Stir into custard mixture; let stand at room temperature until cool.
6 Save 8 whole cherries for garnish in Step 8; chop remaining and stir with orange juice into rice mixture.
7 Beat cream until stiff in a small bowl; fold into rice mixture. Spoon into a buttered 8-cup mold. Chill at least 4 hours or overnight.
8 To unmold, loosen around edge with a knife; shake mold gently to loosen at bottom. Invert onto serving plate; lift off mold carefully. Stuff the saved 8 cherries with slivered almonds; arrange around base of pudding; pile remaining almonds on top.

Strawberry Cheese Mold

Two kinds of cheese make this handsome dessert flavored with berries and lime super smooth

Makes 10 servings.

1 pint strawberries
¾ cup sugar

2 envelopes unflavored gelatin
½ cup cold water
2 teaspoons grated lime rind
3 tablespoons lime juice
½ cup milk
1 container (16 ounces) creamed cottage cheese
8 ounces cream cheese, softened
3 egg whites
FRESH STRAWBERRY SAUCE (recipe follows)

1 Wash and hull strawberries; slice into a large bowl; add ½ cup of the sugar; let stand about 30 minutes, then crush or puree in container of electric blender. Pour back into large bowl.
2 Sprinkle gelatin over cold water in small saucepan; let stand 5 minutes to soften. Heat, stirring constantly, over low heat just until gelatin is dissolved. Stir in lime rind and juice; add to strawberry mixture.
3 Combine milk and cottage cheese in container of electric blender. Whirl at high speed until smooth. Add cream cheese in several pieces; whirl just until smooth. Add to strawberry mixture, stirring until smooth. Chill, stirring often, until mixture mounds slightly when spooned.
4 Beat egg whites until foamy white in small bowl. Gradually beat in remaining ¼ cup sugar, 1 tablespoon at a time, until meringue stands in soft peaks. Fold meringue into cheese mixture. Spoon into an 8-cup mold. Chill at least 4 hours, or until firm.
5 Loosen mold around edge with small knife; dip mold quickly in and out of hot water. Wipe water off mold. Place serving plate over mold; turn upside down; shake mold to release, lift off. Keep refrigerated until serving time.
6 To serve, spoon FRESH STRAWBERRY SAUCE around base of cheese mold; decorate with additional strawberries and lime slices; sprinkle with grated lime rind.

FRESH STRAWBERRY SAUCE
Wash and hull 1 pint strawberries; halve, or slice if large, into a medium-size bowl. Add ¼ cup sugar; toss gently. Let stand 20 to 30 minutes until juices run freely.

Exciting Pastries and Pies

"You can't always tell a book by its cover" is an old saying. And you certainly cannot tell the secret ingredient of many of the pastries and pies in these pages. The delight on the opening picture shouts out strawberries, but look at the chess pies, or some of the meringues, and be excited by the surprise.

SHORTCAKES

Imperial Strawberry Shortcake

The All-American dessert favorite is certainly strawberry shortcake

Bake at 350° for 25 minutes.
Makes 8 servings.

1 cup sifted all-purpose flour
1 teaspoon baking powder
¼ teaspoon salt
⅓ cup milk
2 tablespoons butter or margarine
3 eggs
1 cup sugar
1 teaspoon vanilla
2 pints strawberries
   OR: 1 package (1 pound) frozen unsugared strawberries, thawed
½ to ¾ cup sugar
1 cup heavy cream

1 Sift flour, baking powder and salt onto wax paper.
2 Heat milk with butter just to scalding; cool slightly.
3 Beat eggs until foamy in small bowl with electric mixer. Add the 1 cup sugar gradually until mixture is very thick and fluffy. Add vanilla.
4 Sprinkle flour mixture a third at a time over eggs, alternating with warmed milk and beginning and ending with flour mixture. Pour into two greased and floured 8x1½-inch cake pans (or one 8-inch spring-form pan).
5 Bake in a moderate oven (350°) for 25 minutes (35 minutes for spring-form pan) or until tops spring back when lightly pressed with fingertip. Cool layers on wire rack 10 minutes; loosen around edges with knife; turn out; cool completely.
6 Wash and hull strawberries, reserving a cup for garnish. (For frozen berries, sprinkle with sugar and let stand while defrosting.) Slice remaining berries into a large bowl; add sugar; stir lightly, crushing a few of the berries. Let stand 30 minutes or until juices run freely.
7 Whip cream in small bowl until soft peaks form.
8 Place one cake layer on serving plate (split cake in half if using a spring-form pan). Top with half of the cream and strawberries. Top with remaining cake layer and cream. Place one whole strawberry in center of cake; cut remaining reserved strawberries in half. Arrange halved strawberries cut side up in rosette pattern over the cream.

Strawberry Shortcake Seville

Orange pinwheel biscuits bake in layers to stack warm with sweetened fruit and gobs of whipped cream

Bake at 425° for 25 minutes.
Makes 8 to 10 servings.

3 pints strawberries
¾ cup sugar
4 cups biscuit mix
1⅓ cups milk
2 tablespoons grated orange rind
2 cups cream for whipping
1 tablespoon vanilla

1 Wash strawberries, hull, and slice into a medium-size bowl; sprinkle with ¼ cup of the sugar; toss lightly to mix. Let stand while making shortcake.
2 Prepare biscuit mix with milk, following label directions for rolled biscuits. Roll out half to a

As regal as they come, **Imperial Strawberry Shortcake** is a cook's dream—high in color, texture, and flavor-appeal.

(continued)

There's plenty of flavor in **Strawberry Shortcake Seville** (front) and **Shortcake Compote**—two of America's favorite strawberry desserts.

rectangle, 16x12, on a lightly floured pastry cloth or board.

3 Mix remaining ½ cup sugar and orange rind in a cup; sprinkle half over dough; roll up, jelly-roll fashion. Cut into 16 one-inch-thick slices. Place, cut side down, in a greased baking pan, 8x8x2, to make 4 rows of 4 biscuits each. Repeat with remaining half of dough and sugar mixture, and place in a second baking pan, 8x8x2.

4 Bake in hot oven (425°) 25 minutes, or until golden.

5 Combine cream and vanilla in a medium-size bowl; beat until stiff.

6 Remove biscuits from pans by turning upside down on a wire rack so as not to break layers. Place one layer on a flat serving plate; top with half of the berries, then second shortcake layer and remaining berries. Spoon part of the whipped cream on top and serve remaining separately. To serve shortcake, break apart with two forks.

Shortcake Compote

Scoop the sugary biscuits and fruits into big bowls to enjoy with oodles of cool rich cream

Bake biscuits at 450° for 12 minutes.
Makes 8 to 10 servings.

1 cup sifted all-purpose flour
1¼ teaspoons baking powder
¼ teaspoon salt
⅛ teaspoon baking soda
3 tablespoons vegetable shortening
½ cup buttermilk
1 tablespoon butter or margarine, melted
1 teaspoon sugar
1 pint blueberries
2 pints raspberries
   OR: 2 pints strawberries
1 package (10 ounces) frozen sliced peaches, thawed and drained
   Light cream or table cream

1 Sift flour, baking powder, salt, and soda into a medium-size bowl; cut in shortening with a pastry blender until mixture is crumbly. Add buttermilk all at once; mix lightly just until evenly moist.

2 Turn out onto a lightly floured pastry cloth or board; knead gently ½ minute; pat into a round ¼ inch thick.

3 Cut into small rounds with a floured 1½-inch cutter; place on a greased cookie sheet. Prick tops with a fork; brush with melted butter or

margarine; sprinkle with sugar. Reroll all trimmings; cut out and place on cookie sheet.

4 Bake in very hot oven (450°) 12 minutes, or until golden; remove from cookie sheet; cool on wire racks.

5 Wash blueberries and stem; wash raspberries. If using strawberries, wash, hull, and halve.

6 When ready to serve, layer blueberries, raspberries or strawberries, peaches, and biscuits into a large serving bowl. Garnish with sprigs of mint, if you wish. Spoon into individual serving bowls; serve with cream.

CHESS PIES

Raspberry-Pear Pie

Each fruit complements the other

Bake at 400° for 1 hour.
Makes one 9-inch pie.

6 large fresh pears
1 tablespoon lemon juice
1 package (10 ounces) frozen red raspberries, thawed
1 cup sugar
½ cup sifted all-purpose flour
¼ teaspoon ground cinnamon
1 package piecrust mix
3 tablespoons butter or margarine

1 Pare pears; quarter, core and slice thin into a large bowl. Drizzle lemon juice over top, then toss to coat well; add raspberries and syrup.

2 Mix sugar, flour and cinnamon in a small bowl; sprinkle over fruit mixture; toss to mix well.

3 Prepare piecrust mix, following label directions, or make pastry from your favorite double-crust recipe. Roll out half to a 13-inch round on a lightly floured pastry cloth or board; fit into a deep 9-inch pie plate; trim overhang to ½ inch. Spoon fruit mixture into crust; dot with the butter or margarine.

4 Roll out remaining pastry to an 11-inch round; cut several slits near center to let steam escape; place over filling. Trim overhang to ½ inch; turn edges under, flush with rim; flute to make a stand-up edge. (If you wish to make a rope edge on pie, turn overhang under, flush with rim, then

(continued)

pinch to make a stand-up edge. Press a pencil or skewer diagonally into stand-up edge all the way around to make wide, evenly spaced ridges.)

5 Bake pie in hot oven (400°) 1 hour, or until juices bubble up and pastry is golden. Cool several hours on a wire rack. Garnish with several raspberries and huckleberry leaves, if you wish.

Note—To fix raspberries for garnish, thaw package of fruit called for in recipe just enough to pick out several pretty whole berries. Stand them, not touching, in a small pan; refreeze until time to garnish pie.

Black Walnut Chess Pie

A Southern treat for the Northern family

Bake at 375° for 45 minutes.
Makes one 7½-inch pie.

1 unbaked 7½-inch pastry shell
½ cup (1 stick) butter or margarine, softened
1 cup sugar
3 tablespoons flour
⅛ teaspoon salt
3 egg yolks
1 small can evaporated milk (⅔ cup)
1 teaspoon vanilla
½ cup chopped black walnuts

1 Prepare pastry shell, using your favorite one-crust recipe, or buy a packaged one; chill. Beat butter or margarine and sugar in a medium-size bowl until well mixed. Add flour, salt, egg yolks and evaporated milk. Beat with rotary beater until well mixed. Stir in vanilla and walnuts. Pour mixture into unbaked shell.

2 Bake on lower shelf of a moderate oven (375°) for about 45 minutes or until center is almost set but still soft. Cool thoroughly on wire rack before slicing.

Chocolate Brownie Pie

The favorite brownie in a crust

Bake at 375° for 40 minutes.
Makes one 9-inch pie.

1 unbaked 9-inch pastry shell
2 tablespoons butter or margarine
2 squares unsweetened chocolate
3 eggs

½ cup sugar
¾ cup light corn syrup
1 teaspoon vanilla
¾ cup broken pecans

1 Prepare pastry shell, using your favorite one-crust recipe; chill. Melt butter or margarine and chocolate in a heavy saucepan over low heat. Pour into a medium-size bowl; cool slightly. Add eggs, sugar and corn syrup. Beat with rotary beater until well-blended. Stir in vanilla and pecans. Pour mixture into unbaked shell.

2 Bake on lower shelf of a moderate oven (375°) for 40 minutes. Cool thoroughly on wire rack before slicing. Top with vanilla ice cream or whipped cream, if you wish.

Note: The pastry crust of this pie may "dimple" in several tiny pockets due to the nature of these syrup pies. This won't affect its taste or overall appearance.

French Lemon Pie

The French may not have tasted this one—but you'll still enjoy it

Bake at 375° for 45 minutes.
Makes one 9- or 10-inch pie.

1 unbaked 9- or 10-inch pastry shell
1 cup sugar
3 tablespoons flour
3 eggs
1 cup light corn syrup
¼ cup (½ stick) butter or margarine, melted
2 teaspoons grated lemon rind
3 tablespoons lemon juice
1 lemon, thinly sliced

1 Prepare pastry shell in a 9- or 10-inch fluted tart pan with removable bottom or a regular pie plate, using your favorite one-crust recipe; chill. Mix sugar and flour in a large bowl. Add eggs, syrup and melted butter or margarine; beat with rotary beater until well-mixed. Stir in lemon rind and juice. Pour mixture into unbaked pastry shell. Arrange lemon slices on top.

2 Bake on lower shelf of moderate oven (375°) for 45 minutes or until center is almost set but still soft. Cool thoroughly on wire rack before slicing.

Chess pies have nothing to do with chess, but you'll enjoy the intricate flavors of rich **French Lemon Pie, Chocolate Brownie Pie,** and **Black Walnut Chess Pie.**

Southern Chess Pie

This is a simple pie with an elegant taste

Bake at 375° for 45 minutes.
Makes one 7½-inch pie.

1 unbaked 7½-inch pastry shell
½ cup (1 stick) butter or margarine
1½ cups sugar
3 eggs

1 tablespoon white vinegar
1 teaspoon vanilla

1 Prepare pastry shell, using your favorite one-crust recipe, or buy a packaged one; chill. Heat butter or margarine and sugar in a small saucepan until butter is melted (do not boil); cool slightly.
2 Beat eggs in a large bowl until frothy. Add vinegar, vanilla and butter-sugar mixture; mix well. Pour mixture into unbaked shell.

(continued)

3 Bake on lower shelf of a moderate oven (375°) for about 45 minutes or until center is almost set but still soft. Cool thoroughly on wire rack before cutting.

Strawberry-Nectar Pie

Strawberries blend with apricots for the unusual flavor in this two-layer treat

Bake at 425° for 15 minutes.
Makes one 9-inch pie.

Pastry for a 9-inch single-crust pie
1 can (1 pound, 14 ounces) peeled whole apricots
¼ cup sugar
¼ cup cornstarch
½ teaspoon salt
1 teaspoon lemon juice
Red food coloring
4 cups (2 pints) strawberries, washed and hulled

1 Make pastry with piecrust mix, following label directions, or use your own favorite one-crust recipe. Roll out to a 12-inch round on a lightly floured pastry cloth or board; fit into a 9-inch pie plate. Trim overhang to ½ inch; turn under, flush with rim; flute to make a stand-up edge. Prick shell well all over with a fork.

2 Bake in hot oven (425°) 15 minutes, or until golden; cool completely on a wire rack.

3 Drain syrup from apricots into a small bowl; set aside for Steps 4 and 6. Pit apricots; place apricots in an electric-blender container; cover. Beat at high speed 1 minute, or until smooth. (Or press through a sieve into a small bowl.)

4 Combine sugar, cornstarch and salt in a medium-size saucepan; stir in apricot puree and ¼ cup of the saved apricot syrup.

5 Cook, stirring constantly, until mixture thickens and boils 3 minutes; remove from heat. Stir in lemon juice and a few drops red food coloring to tint a bright pink. Cool 30 minutes.

6 Measure 2 tablespoonfuls into a cup and stir in ¼ cup of the saved apricot syrup from Step 3. Set aside for Step 8.

7 Wash, hull and halve 2 cups (1 pint) of the strawberries; stir into remaining cooled apricot mixture. Spoon into baked pastry shell.

8 Wash and hull remaining 2 cups of strawberries. Save one berry for garnish; halve others lengthwise and arrange, cut side down, in an even layer on top of pie. Spoon apricot mixture from Step 6 over; garnish with the saved whole berry. Serve with PINK WHIPPED CREAM, if you wish.

Note—To make PINK WHIPPED CREAM, add a drop or two red food coloring to cream; beat until stiff.

There's more to **Strawberry Nectar Pie** than appears on the surface. Underneath, there's an apricot filling.

When you bite into **Glazed Ruby Tartlets,** you discover a filling of cream cheese.

Glazed Ruby Tartlets

Each strawberry is a glistening jewel in a crown of golden pastry

Bake at 425° for 10 minutes.
Makes 6 tarts

TART SHELLS
1½ cups sifted all-purpose flour
2 tablespoons sugar
6 tablespoons (¾ stick) butter or margarine
1 egg
1 tablespoon cold water
STRAWBERRY GLAZE
3 cups (from 2 pints) strawberries, washed and hulled
½ cup sugar
2 tablespoons cornstarch
⅛ teaspoon salt
½ cup water
CREAM-CHEESE LAYER
1 package (3 ounces) cream cheese
2 tablespoons 10X (confectioners' powdered) sugar
1 tablespoon cream for whipping

1 Make tart shells: Sift flour and sugar into medium-size bowl; cut in butter or margarine with pastry blender until mixture is crumbly.
2 Beat egg slightly with water in a cup; sprinkle over flour mixture. Mix lightly with a fork until well blended. Turn out onto wax paper; press into a ball.
3 Roll out half of pastry to ⅛-inch thickness on lightly floured pastry cloth or board; cut out three 6-inch rounds. Fit into three 4-inch tart-shell pans, pressing dough firmly against bottoms and sides; prick all over with a fork. Repeat with remaining pastry to make a total of 6 shells.
4 Bake in hot oven (425°) 10 minutes; cool completely on wire rack before removing from pans. (Tart shells can be made ahead, if you wish.)
5 Make strawberry glaze: Pick over and hull strawberries, saving out 30 of the firmest and prettiest for Step 7. Combine sugar, cornstarch and salt in medium-size saucepan; slowly stir in water and remaining berries. Cook over low heat, stirring constantly and mashing berries as they heat, until mixture thickens and boils 3 minutes. Remove from heat; cool slightly.
6 Make cream-cheese layer: Blend all ingredients in a small bowl until mixture is easy to spread.
7 Spread cheese mixture evenly over bottoms of tart shells; fill with saved whole strawberries, standing each tip end up. Spoon cooled strawberry glaze over each; chill 1 hour, or until set.

Mincemeat-Pear Pie

A streusel topping sets off this all-season pie

Bake at 400° for 45 minutes.
Makes one 9-inch pie.

½ package piecrust mix
1 large lemon
3 large fresh pears
1 jar (1 pound, 12 ounces) prepared mincemeat
¾ cup sifted all-purpose flour
¼ cup sugar
½ teaspoon pumpkin-pie spice
¼ cup (½ stick) butter or margarine

1 Prepare piecrust mix, following label directions, or make pastry from your favorite single-

(continued)

A star on any buffet, **Mincemeat-Pear Pie** is topped with a rose
you make from lemon peel.

crust recipe. Roll out to a 12-inch round on a lightly floured pastry cloth or board; fit into a 9-inch pie plate. Trim overhang to ½ inch; turn under, flush with rim; flute to make a stand-up edge.

2 Grate 1 teaspoon lemon peel; reserve. Squeeze lemon; measure 2 tablespoons juice; reserve.

3 Pare pears; quarter and core. Slice 1 of the pears into wedges in a small bowl; sprinkle lemon juice over top, then toss lightly to coat well. Chop remaining pears finely.

4 Combine chopped pears, lemon peel, mincemeat and ¼ cup of the flour in a medium-size bowl. Spoon into prepared pastry shell. Arrange pear wedges on top, pinwheel fashion.

5 Combine remaining ½ cup flour, sugar, and pumpkin-pie spice in a small bowl. Cut in butter or margarine with a pastry blender or two knives until mixture is crumbly. Sprinkle crumbs over top of pie.

6 Bake in hot oven (400°) 45 minutes, or until crumbs are golden-brown and filling is bubbly. Cool completely on a wire rack.

7 Garnish with a lemon rose, if you wish. Choose a medium-size lemon and, starting at the stem end, pare off peel in one continuous long strip. Rewind spiral, following natural curl. Stand on stem end; curl spiral as tight as you wish to resemble opened rose.

Raisin Cream Pie

Plan on 8 servings with this pie—it's lusciously rich!

Bake at 425° for 40 minutes.
Makes one 9-inch pie.

1 package piecrust mix
3 cups seedless raisins
1 cup water
¾ cup firmly packed brown sugar
2 teaspoons cornstarch
½ teaspoon salt
2 teaspoons lemon peel
2 teaspoons lemon juice
½ cup chopped walnuts
1 cup dairy sour cream

1 Prepare piecrust, following label directions; roll out half and line a 9-inch pie plate.

2 Simmer raisins in water 5 minutes; stir in brown sugar, cornstarch and salt, mixed; cook, stirring constantly, 5 minutes.

3 Remove from heat; stir in lemon peel and juice, walnuts and sour cream; spoon into pie shell; cover, crisscross fashion, with ½-inch-wide pastry strips cut from remaining pastry.

4 Bake in hot oven (425°) 40 minutes, or until pastry is golden.

MERINGUES

Orange Pouf Glacé

Here's a real showy holiday dessert to cut in as many as 12 servings—it's that rich!

Bake at 275° for 1 hour, then leave in oven with heat off for 2 hours.
Makes one 9-inch filled meringue.

MERINGUE SHELL
4 egg whites
¼ teaspoon cream of tartar
¼ teaspoon salt
½ teaspoon lemon extract
1 cup sugar

FILLING
4 egg yolks
1 whole egg
⅔ cup sugar
¼ cup frozen concentrated orange juice (from a 6-ounce can)
1 tablespoon lemon juice
1½ cups cream for whipping
Red food coloring

1 Line a large cookie sheet with brown paper; mark an 8-inch circle in middle, using a layer-cake pan as a guide.
2 Make meringue shell: Beat egg whites with cream of tartar, salt, and lemon extract until foamy-white and double in volume in a large bowl. Sprinkle in sugar *very slowly*, 1 tablespoon at a time, beating all the time until sugar dissolves completely and meringue stands in firm peaks. (Beating will take about 25 minutes in all with an electric mixer.)
3 Spread about ¾ of the meringue inside the circle on brown paper, dishing center slightly and making top edge even. (Meringue will spread slightly during baking.)
4 Fit star tip onto a pastry bag; fill with remaining meringue; press out into rosettes all the way around edge of shell. (Or make tiny meringue swirls with tip of teaspoon.) Spread any remaining meringue around inside edge of shell.
5 Bake in very slow oven (275°) 1 hour, or until delicately golden. Turn heat off; leave in oven with door closed 2 hours to crisp. Remove carefully from brown paper with a wide spatula; place on serving plate. (Meringue shell can be made ahead, if you wish. Store in a container with a tight-fitting lid so it will stay crisp.)
6 Make filling: Beat egg yolks and whole egg slightly in top of a small double boiler; stir in

sugar, concentrated orange juice, and lemon juice. Cook, stirring constantly, over simmering water 10 minutes, or until thick. Strain into a medium-size bowl; set in a large bowl of ice and water. Chill, stirring several times, 10 minutes, or until very thick.
7 While custard chills, beat 1 cup of the cream until stiff in a small bowl. (Save remaining cream for next step.) Fold into orange-juice mixture, still keeping bowl over ice, until no streaks of white or yellow remain. Pile into meringue shell. Chill 2 hours, or until softly set. (Pudding will mound slightly when dropped from a spoon.)
8 Just before serving, beat saved ½ cup cream until stiff in a small bowl; tint delicate pink with red food coloring. Spoon in big puffs on top of filling. Cut meringue into thin wedges.

TIPS FOR PERFECT MERINGUES

- *Choose a cool dry day, for humid air tends to soften meringues. Be sure your tools—bowl and beater—are clean and dry. The tiniest speck of fat will spoil meringues.*
- *Egg whites will beat higher if allowed to stand at room temperature to warm slightly but eggs separate best when cold.*
- *Make your electric mixer your right arm, for long beating is a must to dissolve sugar completely and prevent meringue from "weeping." To test if sugar is dissolved: Rub a bit of meringue between your fingers. It should feel perfectly smooth—not grainy.*

Peach Meringue Crown

When it's peach season, this is the ideal dessert—peaches in the sauce and on top of the ice cream

Bake twice at 250° for 45 minutes.
Makes 12 servings.

6 egg whites
1¾ cups sugar
1 quart vanilla ice cream
3 large ripe peaches, peeled, halved, and pitted
ALMOND PEACH GLAZE *(recipe follows)*
(continued)

1 Line a cookie sheet with brown paper; draw a 7-inch circle in center, using a bowl or salad plate as a guide.

2 Make meringue in two batches: Beat 3 egg whites until foamy-white and double in volume in a medium-size bowl. Sprinkle in 1 cup of the sugar *very slowly,* 1 tablespoon at a time, beating all the time until sugar dissolves completely and meringue stands in firm peaks.

3 Spread mixture inside the outline on brown paper, building up a 2-inch rim around edge.

4 Bake in very slow oven (250°) 45 minutes, or until firm. Let cool on paper while making second batch of meringue.

5 Beat remaining 3 egg whites with remaining ¾ cup sugar, following directions in Steps 2 and 3.

6 Fit a large star tip onto a pastry bag and fill with meringue mixture. Pipe rings around side and on top of baked meringue rim; make swirls around top with remaining meringue.

7 Bake "decorated" meringue in very slow oven (250°) 45 minutes, or until firm. Cool completely on paper, then loosen shell with a spatula. (This can be done several days before serving; simply store meringue shell in a container with a tight-fitting lid.)

8 One hour before serving: Place meringue shell on a serving plate. Scoop ice cream with large spoon to make "petals" and fill meringue shell. Arrange peach halves over ice cream; top with ALMOND PEACH GLAZE.

ALMOND PEACH GLAZE

Mash 1 peeled, halved, and pitted ripe peach in a small saucepan; stir in ½ cup light corn syrup. Heat to boiling; reduce heat; simmer 5 minutes. Remove from heat; stir in ½ teaspoon almond extract. Cool. Makes about 1 cup.

Meringue Shells

You'll find dozens of uses for them

Bake at 275° for 45 minutes.
Makes 8 four-inch shells.

3 egg whites
½ teaspoon cream of tartar
⅛ teaspoon salt
½ teaspoon vanilla
¾ cup sugar

1 Combine egg whites, cream of tartar, salt, and vanilla in your biggest bowl. Start mixer at me-

dium speed and beat for 2 minutes, or just until mixture turns foamy-white and doubles in volume.

2 Increase speed—just enough so sugar won't fly. Start sprinkling it in *very slowly* as beater whirls. It'll take 15 minutes. Switch to high; beat 10 minutes longer to dissolve every grain of sugar.

3 Ready a brown-paper-lined cookie sheet marked with 8 four-inch circles. Spoon on meringue and swirl into shells. Bake in very slow oven (275°) 45 minutes, or until set. Cool; peel off paper.

Apple-Mint Charlotte

Pastel green, a springtime dessert for any time of year

Makes 8 servings.

10 ladyfingers
 2 envelopes unflavored gelatin
 1 cup apple juice
 3 eggs, separated
 1 can or jar (about 1 pound) applesauce
 ½ teaspoon mint extract
   Green and blue food colorings
 1 package (3 ounces) whipped topping mix
   Milk
   Vanilla
 ¼ teaspoon cream of tartar
 ⅓ cup sugar

1 Separate ladyfingers; stand around edge in an 8-inch spring-form pan to line completely.

2 Soften gelatin in apple juice in the top of a double boiler. Beat in egg yolks and applesauce.

3 Cook over simmering water 15 minutes, or until gelatin dissolves and mixture thickens slightly; pour into a large bowl. Stir in mint extract and a few drops each green and blue colorings to tint deep green.

4 Place bowl in a pan of ice and water to speed setting. Chill, stirring several times, just until as thick as unbeaten egg white.

5 While gelatin mixture chills, prepare topping mix with milk and vanilla, following label directions. Beat egg whites with cream of tartar until foamy-white and double in volume in a medium-size bowl; beat in sugar, 1 tablespoon at a time, until sugar dissolves and meringue stands in firm peaks.

6 Fold whipped topping, then meringue into thickened gelatin mixture until no streaks of

Peach Meringue Crown is a stunning example of creative dessert-making that anyone will be proud to display.

white remain. Spoon into prepared pan, making deep swirls on top. Chill several hours, or until firm.

7 When ready to serve, release spring and carefully lift off side of pan; slide dessert, on its metal base, onto a serving plate. Garnish with more whipped topping and mint candies, if you wish.

Memorable Puddings

Tired of serving up the same old pudding? Then try one of the many exciting puddings in these pages. From custards, souffles, cremes, and puddings, there are recipes that you'll enjoy putting together—and best of all, that your friends and family will ask for again.

CUSTARDS

Eggs in Snow

Fluffy little islands of meringue with candied orange topping turn a simple soft custard into an elegant dessert

Makes 6 servings.

SOFT CUSTARD
1 large navel orange
2 cups milk
3 egg yolks
2 whole eggs
¼ cup sugar
1 teaspoon vanilla
2 tablespoons Grand Marnier
    OR: 2 tablespoons frozen orange juice concentrate

MERINGUE
3 egg whites
6 tablespoons sugar
Candied Orange Rind (recipe follows)

1 Make SOFT CUSTARD: Pare orange thinly with vegetable parer, cutting only the bright orange part and none of the white. Reserve rind and the orange.
2 Scald milk with a 3-inch piece of orange rind in top of a double-boiler placed over direct heat. Beat egg yolks, eggs, and ¼ cup sugar with wire whisk or rotary beater until light and fluffy; gradually stir in scalded milk; pour mixture back into top of double-boiler.
3 Cook, stirring constantly, over simmering water 10 minutes or until custard thickens

slightly. Remove from heat; strain into a small bowl; stir in vanilla and Grand Marnier. Cover; chill.
4 Make MERINGUES: Heat 1 quart lightly salted water just to simmering in large skillet.
5 Beat egg whites in medium-size bowl with electric mixer until foamy-white and double in volume. Beat in 6 tablespoons sugar, 1 at a time, until meringue stands in firm peaks.
6 Scoop meringue with large spoon into 6 large egg-shaped puffs. Float, not touching, on simmering water; cover skillet. Cook over very low heat 5 minutes. Lift from water with slotted spoon; drain on cookie sheet covered with paper toweling; chill.
7 To serve: Pare all white from reserved orange and cut orange into thin slices. Press slices against side of shallow glass bowl; carefully pour in custard sauce. Float meringue islands gently on top; spoon a little CANDIED ORANGE RIND and syrup over each.

CANDIED ORANGE RIND
Cut the remaining rind removed from the orange into match-like strips. Simmer in water 5 minutes; drain. Combine ½ cup sugar and ¼ cup water in small saucepan; bring to boiling, stirring constantly until sugar is melted. Boil 2 minutes; add orange rind; continue cooking 5 minutes. Cool completely. When covered, will keep in refrigerator several weeks.

Pots de Crème au Chocolat

This rich, satiny dessert is traditionally baked and served in pot de crème cups—but custard cups or individual soufflé dishes will serve as nicely

Bake at 325° for 20 minutes.
Makes 4 to 6 servings.

4 squares semi-sweet chocolate
1¼ cups light or heavy cream
3 egg yolks
2 tablespoons light brown sugar

1 Place four 4-ounce or six 3-ounce pots de crème cups, custard cups or individual soufflé dishes in shallow baking dish.

(continued)

You'd never believe they're custards, but **Eggs in Snow, Pots de Creme au Chocolat, Cinnamon-Raisin Bread Pudding** (center), and **Maurice Moore-Betty's Trifle** (top) are just that.

2 Chop the chocolate coarsely. Place in small heavy saucepan; add cream. Cook, stirring constantly, over medium-high heat, until chocolate melts and mixture comes to boiling.
3 Beat egg yolks and sugar with wire whisk in medium-size bowl until blended; gradually beat in ½ cup hot cream mixture, then slowly add the rest. Strain into 4-cup measure; pour into cups.
4 Set shallow baking pan on oven rack. Pour boiling water into pan, about half way up the sides of cups.
5 Bake in slow oven (325°) for 20 minutes or just until mixture begins to set around edges. Remove cups from water to a wire rack; let cool 30 minutes. Cover with lids or plastic wrap; refrigerate at least 4 hours. Decorate with rosettes of whipped cream and candied lilacs, if you wish.

Cinnamon-Raisin Bread Pudding

Bread puddings were invented by our thrifty ancestors to make good use of stale bread. If you can't wait for your bread to become stale, follow our directions for drying fresh bread.

Bake at 350° for 50 minutes.
Makes 6 to 8 servings.

 8 to 10 slices firm white bread
 ¼ cup (½ stick) butter or margarine, melted
 ½ cup light or dark raisins
 ¾ cup sugar
 1 teaspoon ground cinnamon
 ¼ teaspoon salt
 4 eggs
 4 cups milk
 1 teaspoon vanilla
 ¼ cup apple jelly

1 If bread is very fresh, place in single layer on cookie sheet to dry out for about 1 hour at room temperature. Brush one side of each slice with melted butter; cut into quarters. Arrange bread, over-lapping, in shallow 2-quart baking dish; sprinkle with raisins. Mix sugar and cinnamon; sprinkle half over bread.
2 Combine remaining sugar-cinnamon mixture, salt and eggs in large bowl; beat with wire whisk or rotary beater, just until combined. Stir in milk and vanilla; ladle over bread.
3 Set baking dish in a shallow pan; place pan on oven shelf; pour boiling water into pan to a depth of 1 inch.
4 Bake in moderate oven (350°) for 50 minutes

or until center is almost set, but still soft; remove baking dish from water to a wire rack.
5 Melt apple jelly in small saucepan; brush over top of bread pudding. Serve hot or warm; pass cream to pour over each serving, if you wish.

Maurice Moore-Betty's Trifle

This recipe was originally devised to use up stale cake, which is delicious after it soaks up the custard and sherry

Makes 8 servings.

 1¾ cups milk
 1 three-inch piece vanilla bean, split
  OR: 1 teaspoon vanilla
 5 egg yolks
 ½ cup sugar
 1 recipe Sponge Cake (recipe follows) (make at least 2 days ahead)
 ½ cup raspberry preserves
 ½ to 1 cup dry sherry
 1 cup heavy cream
 2 tablespoons Cognac
 ¼ cup sliced or slivered almonds, toasted
  Angelica (optional)

1 Heat milk with vanilla bean, if used, to scalding in top of double-boiler placed over direct heat.
2 Beat egg yolks and sugar with wire whisk or rotary beater until light and fluffy in medium-size bowl; slowly stir in 1 cup scalded milk; pour all back into top of double boiler.
3 Cook, stirring constantly, over simmering water 10 minutes or until custard thickens slightly and coats the spoon; remove from heat; stir in vanilla, if used. Strain into a clean bowl; cool, stirring often to prevent skin from forming; chill.
4 Split cake horizontally. Spread each half generously with raspberry preserves and sandwich together again. Slice crosswise into ½-inch-thick slices. Press enough slices against side and bottom of a 2-quart serving bowl to line bowl completely. Sprinkle with some of the sherry; arrange remaining slices in center, sprinkling each layer with sherry to soak thoroughly.
5 Beat ½ cup of the cream until it holds soft peaks; fold into custard with Cognac. Pour over sponge cake; chill several hours. Just before serving, beat remaining cream until stiff; spoon over trifle or pipe from a pastry bag with a star tip. Sprinkle almonds over top; decorate with slivers of angelica.

Sponge Cake

Bake at 350° for 40 minutes.
Makes 1 loaf cake.

¾ cup sifted cake flour
¾ cup sugar
¼ teaspoon salt
4 eggs, separated
½ teaspoon cream of tartar
2 tablespoons lemon juice
1 tablespoon water
1 teaspoon vanilla

1 Sift flour, ½ cup of the sugar, and salt onto wax paper.
2 Beat egg whites with cream of tartar in large bowl with electric beater at high speed, until foamy-white and double in volume. Gradually beat in remaining ¼ cup sugar, 1 tablespoon at a time; beat until meringue stands in firm peaks when beaters are slowly raised.
3 With same beaters, beat egg yolks, lemon juice, water and vanilla in small bowl 5 minutes or until light and fluffy.
4 Fold flour mixture, ⅓ at a time, into egg yolk mixture until completely blended. Fold into meringue until no streaks of white and yellow remain. Pour into ungreased 9x5x3-inch loaf pan; smooth top.
5 Bake in slow oven (350°) 40 minutes or until top springs back when lightly pressed with fingertip. Invert pan; rest edges on 2 measuring cups or heavy cans; cool completely. Loosen cake around sides with spatula; carefully remove from pan.

Perfect Custard

You'll find out why they're perfect!

Bake at 325° for 30 minutes.
Makes 8 cup custards.

4 eggs
1 teaspoon vanilla
⅓ cup sugar
Dash of salt
3 cups milk, scalded
Nutmeg, if you like

1 Put eggs and vanilla in a bowl. Beat in sugar and salt just until mixed—no more. Stir in milk. (It's scalded when bubbles form around the edge of pan).

2 Pour through a sieve into eight 5-ounce custard cups—no buttering needed. Sprinkle lightly with nutmeg, then place cups, not touching, in shallow baking pan.
3 Pull out oven shelf a little and set pan on it for easy handling. Pour boiling water from kettle into the pan to make a depth of about 1 inch around the cups.
4 Let them bake lazily in a slow oven (325°) 30 minutes or until centers are almost set but still soft. (Do not overbake; custards will set as they cool.) Lift cups from water; cool.

Caramel Cups

Custard bakes in cups coated with caramel, turns out to make its own sauce!

Bake at 325° for 50 minutes.
Makes 6 servings.

1 cup sugar
6 tablespoons water
2½ cups milk
6 eggs
2 egg yolks
¼ teaspoon salt

1 Combine ½ cup of the sugar and 4 tablespoons of the water in a small heavy saucepan. Heat slowly to boiling, then cook, without stirring, just until mixture turns golden. (Watch carefully, for it will caramelize quickly.) *Very slowly* stir in remaining 2 tablespoons water.
2 Pour about 1 tablespoonful of the hot caramel mixture into each of six 6-ounce custard cups. Tip and turn cups quickly to coat bottom and sides thinly. Let stand while preparing custard.
3 Heat milk very slowly to scalding in a medium-size saucepan.
4 Beat whole eggs and egg yolks slightly in a large bowl; stir in remaining ½ cup sugar and salt; slowly stir in scalded milk. Strain into a 4-cup measure; pour into caramel-coated cups.
5 Set cups in a large pan; place on oven shelf; pour boiling water into pan to within 1 inch of top of cups.
6 Bake in slow oven (325°) 50 minutes, or until center is almost set but still soft. (Do not overbake; custard will set as it cools.) Remove cups from water; cool. Chill at least 4 hours, or overnight.
7 To unmold, loosen custards around edges with a small knife; invert onto dessert plates. (Shake cups, if needed, to loosen custards at bottom.) Garnish each with fresh or thawed frozen peach slices, if you wish.

When you want to go regal, look to **Custard Crown** (top), and as a side dessert add **Caramel Cups.**

Custard Crown

A majestic mold lavish with ladyfingers and candied fruit, ribboned with whipped cream

Bake at 325° for 2 hours.
Makes 8 servings.

¼ cup golden raisins
1 jar (4 ounces) chopped candied pineapple
¼ cup apricot preserves
2 packages (3 ounces each) ladyfingers

6 eggs
½ cup sugar (for custard)
2½ cups milk
¼ cup Cointreau
1 cup cream for whipping
2 tablespoons sugar (for cream)
1 teaspoon vanilla

1 Place raisins in a small saucepan; cover with water. Heat to boiling; remove from heat. Let stand 5 minutes; drain.
2 Chop raisins with pineapple and preserves until almost smooth and pastelike.

3 Butter a straight-side 6-cup mold; line bottom with wax paper. Separate ladyfingers; lay enough in mold to cover bottom; spread with 3 tablespoons of the fruit mixture. (A spoon makes the job go fast.) Stand more ladyfingers, touching each other and rounded sides out, around side of mold to line completely.
4 Beat eggs slightly in a medium-size bowl; stir in the ½ cup sugar, milk, and Cointreau.
5 Ladle 1 cup of the custard mixture into mold. Top with another layer of ladyfingers, spread with 3 tablespoons fruit mixture, and pour in ½ cup custard mixture. Continue layering with remaining ladyfingers and fruit and custard mixtures until all are used.
6 Cover mold with foil, transparent wrap, or double-thick wax paper; tie with string to hold tightly.
7 Set mold in a large pan; place on oven shelf; pour boiling water into pan to within 1 inch of top of mold.
8 Bake in slow oven (325°) 2 hours, or until firm on top. Cool on a wire rack 1 hour, then chill at least 4 hours, or even overnight.
9 To unmold, loosen dessert around edge with a small knife; invert onto a serving plate; lift off mold.
10 Beat cream with the 2 tablespoons sugar and vanilla until stiff in a medium-size bowl. Fit a fancy tip onto a pastry bag; spoon whipped cream into bag. Press out in ribbons around side of mold and in circles of rosettes on top, building up to a peak. Garnish with a tiny wedge of green candied pineapple, if you wish.

SOUFFLES

Regal Hot Chocolate Soufflé

Velvety and warm, an appropriate winter dessert

Bake at 350° for 50 minutes.
Makes 6 servings.

1 cup milk
⅓ cup sugar
2 squares unsweetened chocolate
1 teaspoon vanilla
2 tablespoons butter or margarine
3 tablespoons all-purpose flour
¼ teaspoon salt

6 egg whites
4 egg yolks

1 Coat a 5-cup soufflé dish well with softened butter or margarine; dust evenly with sugar, tapping out excess.
2 Combine milk and sugar in a small saucepan; heat slowly until bubbles appear around edge. Add chocolate; continue heating, stirring constantly, until chocolate is melted. Remove from heat; stir in vanilla.
3 Melt butter or margarine in a medium-size saucepan; blend in flour and salt; slowly stir in chocolate mixture; cook over low heat, stirring constantly, until mixture thickens and bubbles 1 minute. Cool slightly while beating eggs.
4 Beat egg whites in a medium-size bowl, just until soft peaks form.
5 Beat egg yolks well in a large bowl; slowly stir in thickened chocolate mixture. Fold in beaten egg whites until no streaks of white remain. Gently spoon mixture into prepared soufflé dish. Place dish in baking pan on oven rack; pour boiling water into pan to depth of 1 inch.
6 Bake in moderate oven (350°) 50 minutes, or until puffy-light and firm in center. Serve immediately, with cream, if you wish.

Cherry Cordial Chocolate Soufflé

Homemade chocolate cordial cherries add a touch of elegance to this heavenly chocolate soufflé

Makes 10 servings.

1 tablespoon brandy or rum
10 maraschino cherries with stems
8 eggs
1 envelope unflavored gelatin
¼ cup water
1 cup milk
½ cup sugar
½ teaspoon salt
8 squares semisweet chocolate
1 teaspoon rum extract
Whipped cream

1 Pour brandy or rum over cherries in a small bowl; place in freezer, turning cherries a few times, 1 hour.
2 Prepare an ungreased 5- or 6-cup soufflé dish this way: Fold a piece of wax paper, 25 inches long, in half lengthwise; wrap around dish to make a 3-inch stand-up collar; hold in place with string and a paper clip.
3 Soften gelatin in water in a cup.

(continued)

4 Heat milk slowly in a medium-size saucepan until bubbles start to appear around the edge.
5 Separate eggs, putting whites in a large bowl and yolks in a medium-size bowl. Beat yolks slightly with ¼ cup of the sugar and salt. Pour ½ cup of the hot milk into the yolks, beating constantly; return all of the mixture to saucepan.
6 Cook over low heat, stirring constantly, until custard starts to thicken and coats a spoon;

remove from heat. Stir in softened gelatin, until melted; add rum extract. Strain back into medium-size bowl.
7 Melt chocolate squares in a small bowl over hot water.
8 Remove cherries from brandy; holding by the stem, dip one at a time into melted chocolate to coat completely. Place on wax paper; refrigerate.

Chocolate-covered cherries top **Cherry Cordial Chocolate Souffle,** for a custard-dessert that will have them calling for more.

9 Add remaining chocolate and brandy from cherries to yolk mixture; beat until smooth; set bowl in a larger bowl partly filled with ice and water; chill at room temperature, stirring often, just until as thick as unbeaten egg white.

10 While mixture chills, beat egg whites until foamy-white and double in volume. Add remaining ¼ cup sugar slowly, 1 tablespoon at a time, beating until meringue stands in firm peaks.

11 Beat about ¼ of the meringue into thickened chocolate mixture. Fold remaining meringue into chocolate until no streaks of white remain. Spoon into prepared soufflé dish. Chill several hours, or until firm.

12 Just before serving, carefully remove collar; garnish with whipped cream or thawed frozen whipped topping and the chocolate cordial cherries.

Cool Lemon Cream Soufflé

Tart and tangy—a good choice after duck or other rich entrées

Makes 10 servings.

    2 envelopes unflavored gelatin
    1 cup sugar
    6 eggs, separated
    1¼ cups water
    1 tablespoon grated lemon rind
    ½ cup lemon juice
    1½ cups cream for whipping

1 Prepare a 4-cup soufflé or straight-side baking dish this way: Cut two strips of wax paper 12 inches wide and long enough to go around dish with a 1-inch overlap; fold in half lengthwise. Wrap around dish to make a 2-inch stand-up collar; hold in place with cellophane tape or a rubber band and a paper clip.

2 Mix gelatin and ¾ cup of the sugar in a medium-size saucepan; beat in egg yolks until fluffy-light, then water.

3 Cook slowly, stirring constantly, until gelatin dissolves completely and mixture thickens; remove from heat. Pour into a large bowl; stir in lemon rind and juice.

4 Place bowl in a pan of ice and water to speed setting. Chill, stirring often, just until as thick as unbeaten egg white.

5 While gelatin mixture chills, beat egg whites until foamy-white in a medium-size bowl. Beat in remaining ¼ cup sugar, 1 tablespoon at a

time, until meringue forms soft peaks. Beat cream until stiff in a medium-size bowl.

6 Fold meringue, then whipped cream, into thickened lemon mixture. Spoon into prepared dish.

7 Chill several hours, or until firm. Serve plain, or garnish with more whipped cream, sprigs of mint, and a lemon rose, if you wish. (To make a lemon rose: Choose a medium-size lemon, and, starting at the blossom end, peel off rind in one continuous long strip. Wind strip round and round to form a rose pattern.)

Hot Lemon Soufflé

Serve this beauty oven-hot in all its glory. Flavor is tart and so refreshing

Bake at 350° for 50 minutes.
Makes 8 servings.

    3 tablespoons butter or margarine
    3 tablespoons all-purpose flour
    ⅛ teaspoon salt
    ½ cup sugar
    ½ cup water
    ¾ teaspoon grated lemon rind
    ¼ cup lemon juice
    6 eggs, separated

1 Melt butter or margarine in a medium-size saucepan; stir in flour and salt; cook, stirring constantly, just until bubbly.

2 Stir in ¼ cup of the sugar and water; continue cooking and stirring until sauce thickens and boils 1 minute; remove from heat. Stir in lemon rind and juice; let cool while beating eggs.

3 Beat egg whites until foamy-white and double in volume in a large bowl; beat in remaining ¼ cup sugar, 1 tablespoon at a time, beating all the time until meringue forms soft peaks.

4 Beat egg yolks until creamy-thick in a second large bowl; blend in cooled lemon sauce; fold in meringue until no streaks of white remain. Spoon into an ungreased 8-cup soufflé or straight-side baking dish.

5 Set soufflé dish in a baking pan on oven shelf; pour boiling water into pan to depth of about an inch.

6 Bake in moderate oven (350°) 50 minutes, or until puffy-firm and golden on top. Spoon into dessert dishes; serve at once.

Give your guests a choice with **Hot Lemon Souffle** (top) or the bracingly cold
Cafe Cream Cups.

Café Cream Cups

Espresso coffee blends with whipped cream for
these little rich-rich molded soufflés

Makes 6 servings.

2 eggs, separated
½ cup sugar
2 tablespoons instant espresso coffee powder
¼ teaspoon ground cinnamon
1⅓ cups milk
1 envelope unflavored gelatin
½ teaspoon rum flavoring or extract
1 cup cream for whipping

1 Prepare 6 demitasses this way: Cut a 6-inch-
wide piece of foil for each cup and fold in half
lengthwise; wrap around cup, overlapping ends,
to make a 2-inch stand-up collar. Mold foil
tightly at handle; fasten top with a paper clip
and bottom with cellophane tape.

2 Beat egg yolks slightly in the top of a small
double boiler; stir in ¼ cup of the sugar, espresso coffee, cinnamon, and milk; sprinkle
gelatin over to soften. (Set remaining sugar
aside for Step 5.)

3 Cook gelatin mixture, stirring constantly, over
simmering water 10 minutes, or until gelatin
dissolves and mixture thickens slightly; remove
from heat.

4 Strain into a medium-size bowl; stir in rum
flavoring or extract. Set bowl in a larger bowl
partly filled with ice and water to speed setting.
Chill, stirring often, at room temperature just
until as thick as unbeaten egg white.

5 While mixture chills, beat egg whites until
foamy-white and double in volume in a small
bowl; sprinkle in remaining ¼ cup sugar, 1

tablespoon at a time, beating all the time until sugar dissolves and meringue stands in firm peaks. Beat cream until stiff in a medium-size bowl.

6 Fold meringue, then whipped cream into thickened gelatin mixture until no streaks of white remain. Spoon into prepared cups, dividing evenly. Chill several hours, or until firm.

7 When ready to serve, carefully remove foil collars; garnish each souffle with chocolate curls, if you wish. (To make, shave thin strips from a square of unsweetened chocolate with a vegetable parer or sharp knife.)

CRÈMES

Café Cream Royale

It's such a lusciously rich way to enjoy coffee, cream, and chocolate

Makes 8 servings.

6 *eggs, separated*
¾ *cup sugar*
   Dash of salt
2 *cups warm freshly brewed coffee*
2 *envelopes unflavored gelatin*
3 *tablespoons light rum*
1 *cup cream for whipping*
   CANDY CUTOUTS *(recipe follows)*

1 Beat egg yolks slightly in the top of a double boiler; stir in ¼ cup of the sugar, salt, and coffee; sprinkle gelatin over top; let stand several minutes to soften gelatin.

2 Cook, stirring constantly, over simmering water 10 minutes, or until gelatin dissolves and mixture coats a spoon; remove from heat. Strain into a large bowl; stir in rum.

3 Place bowl in a pan of ice and water to speed setting. Chill, stirring often, just until as thick as unbeaten egg white.

4 While gelatin mixture chills, beat egg whites until foamy-white and double in volume in a medium-size bowl; beat in remaining ½ cup sugar, 1 tablespoon at a time, until sugar dissolves completely and meringue stands in firm peaks. Beat cream until stiff in a medium-size bowl.

5 Fold meringue, then whipped cream into thickened gelatin mixture until no streaks of white remain. Spoon into an 8-cup mold. Chill at least 6 hours, or until firm. (Overnight is even better.)

6 When ready to unmold, run a sharp-tip thin-blade knife around top of dessert, then dip mold *very quickly* in and out of a pan of hot water. Cover with a serving plate; turn upside down; gently lift off mold. Trim with CANDY CUTOUTS.

CANDY CUTOUTS

Melt ⅓ semisweet-chocolate pieces with 1 teaspoon shortening in a cup over simmering water. Pour onto a foil-lined cookie sheet; spread into a thin 6x6-inch layer. Chill 15 minutes, or until almost firm; cut into small fancy shapes of your choice with a truffle cutter. Chill again until firm. Carefully peel off foil and lift out cutouts with the tip of a knife.

Honey-Spice Yule Logs

Cake is made like a jelly roll, then filled with whipped cream and frosted with rich coffee-butter icing

Bake at 350° for 8 to 10 minutes.
Makes 6 servings.

⅔ *cup sifted all-purpose flour*
½ *teaspoon baking soda*
½ *teaspoon salt*
½ *teaspoon ground cinnamon*
¼ *teaspoon ground ginger*
⅛ *teaspoon ground cardamom*
3 *tablespoons honey*
2 *tablespoons sugar*
½ *teaspoon lemon juice*
1 *egg, beaten*
1 *cup cream for whipping*
   COFFEE BUTTER CREAM *(recipe follows)*

1 Grease a baking pan, 15x10x1; line with wax paper; grease paper.

2 Measure flour, soda, salt, cinnamon, ginger, and cardamom into sifter.

3 Heat honey *just to lukewarm* in a medium-size saucepan; remove from heat. Stir in sugar and

(continued)

lemon juice, then beaten egg. Sift in dry ingredients and stir until smooth. Spread in prepared pan. (Layer will be thin.)

4 Bake in moderate oven (350°) 8 to 10 minutes, or until top springs back when lightly pressed with fingertip.

5 Invert cake onto a large sheet of wax paper sprinkled lightly with sugar; peel off wax-paper liner and discard. Cut cake and sugared paper in half crosswise. (Use sharp scissors for a quick neat cut.) Starting at a 10-inch end of each, roll up both cakes along with wax paper, jelly-roll fashion. Cool completely on a wire rack.

6 When ready to fill, beat cream until stiff in a medium-size bowl. Unroll cakes, one at a time, and discard wax paper. Spread cakes with whipped cream, then reroll and trim ends.

7 Frost tops and sides with COFFEE BUTTER CREAM; cut each roll into three 3-inch-long logs. Decorate with tiny "holly sprigs" cut from candied citron and candied cherries, and slivered pistachio nuts, if you wish.

Chill until serving time.

COFFEE BUTTER CREAM

Cream ½ cup (1 stick) butter or margarine with ¾ cup sifted 10X (confectioners' powdered) sugar until fluffy in a small bowl. Dissolve 1 tablespoon instant coffee powder in 1 tablespoon hot water in a cup; beat into creamed mixture until it is fluffy-smooth. Makes about 1 cup.

Nesselrode Cream Mold

It's as merry as a holiday package, with its "bowknot" topper and bright fruits peeking through rich cream

Makes 8 to 10 servings.

2 envelopes unflavored gelatin
½ teaspoon salt
⅔ cup sugar
4 eggs, separated
1½ cups milk
1 cup cream for whipping
½ cup bottled nesselrode dessert sauce
2 tablespoons chopped green maraschino cherries

2 tablespoons chopped red maraschino cherries
1 teaspoon vanilla

1 Mix gelatin, salt, and ⅓ cup of the sugar in a cup. (Set remaining ⅓ cup sugar aside for Step 3.) Beat egg yolks with milk until blended in top of a small double boiler; sprinkle in gelatin mixture.

2 Cook, stirring constantly, over hot, *not boiling*, water 15 minutes, or until gelatin dissolves and mixture coats a metal spoon; strain into a medium-size bowl. Chill, stirring often, 50 minutes, or until as thick as unbeaten egg white.

3 Beat egg whites until foamy-white and double in volume in a large bowl; beat in remaining ⅓ cup sugar, a tablespoon at a time, until meringue forms soft peaks. Beat ½ cup of the cream until stiff in a small bowl. (Remaining cream is for topping in Step 7.)

4 Place bowl of meringue in a deep pan partly filled with ice and water to speed setting. Fold in thickened gelatin mixture, then whipped cream, nesselrode sauce, cherries, and vanilla.

5 Continue folding, keeping bowl over ice, until no streaks of white remain and mixture mounds on a spoon. Spoon into an 8-cup mold. Chill several hours, or until firm. (Overnight is better.)

6 When ready to serve, run a sharp-tip thin-blade knife around top of mold, then dip mold *very quickly* in and out of a pan of hot water. Cover mold with a serving plate; turn upside down; carefully lift off mold.

7 Beat remaining ½ cup cream until stiff in a small bowl; spoon in puffs on top. Or spoon cream into a pastry bag, and, using a fancy tip, press out in shape of bow. Decorate plate with holly, if you wish.

Creme Brulée

French classic with an unusual ending—fast broiling with the dish set in ice

Bake at 300° for 1 hour and 15 minutes.
Makes 4 servings.

2 cups light cream or table cream
¼ cup granulated sugar
¼ teaspoon salt
2 eggs
1½ teaspoons vanilla
2 tablespoons brown sugar

1 Heat cream to scalding in top of a double boiler over simmering water; stir in granulated sugar and salt; remove from heat.

Match your dessert with the season, and you'll have a winner, like **Honey-Spice Yule Log** or **Nesselrode Cream Mold,** two reflections of winter.

2 Beat eggs slightly in a medium-size bowl; slowly stir in scalded cream mixture and vanilla. Strain into a broilerproof shallow 3-cup baking dish.

3 Set dish in a large pan; place on oven shelf; pour boiling water into pan to within 1 inch of top of dish.

4 Bake in slow oven (300°) 1 hour and 15 minutes, or until center is almost set but still soft.

(continued)

(Do not overbake; custard will set as it cools.) Remove from water; cool; chill.

5 Just before serving, press brown sugar through a sieve on top of chilled custard. Place dish in a pan of ice. Broil 3 to 4 minutes, or until sugar starts to melt and bubble up. Spoon into dessert dishes.

Mexican Creme

Coffee and spice blend with cream to give this handsome mold a tropical flavor

Makes 8 servings

½ cup sugar
1 envelope unflavored gelatin
1½ teaspoons instant coffee powder
¼ teaspoon ground cinnamon
⅛ teaspoon salt
½ teaspoon vanilla
2 eggs
1¼ cups milk
1 cup cream for whipping

1 Combine ¼ cup sugar, gelatin, instant coffee, cinnamon, salt, and vanilla in top of double boiler. (Save remaining ¼ cup sugar for Step 4.)
2 Separate eggs, putting whites in medium-size bowl, yolks in small bowl. Beat egg yolks slightly; stir in milk; stir into gelatin mixture.
3 Cook over simmering water, stirring constantly, 5 minutes, or until gelatin dissolves and mixture coats a metal spoon; strain into small bowl. Chill, stirring occasionally, until mixture is as thick as unbeaten egg whites.
4 Beat egg whites until foamy-white and double in volume; gradually beat in saved ¼ cup sugar; 1 tablespoon at a time, beating well after each, until meringue stands in firm peaks. Beat cream until stiff in small bowl.
5 Place bowl of meringue in pan of ice and water. Gradually fold in gelatin mixture, then whipped cream. Continue folding, keeping bowl over ice, until no streaks of white remain and mixture holds its shape.
6 Pour into 6-cup mold; chill 4 hours, or until firm.
7 Unmold onto serving plate. Garnish with whipped cream and shaved semisweet chocolate, if you wish.

PUDDINGS

Party Trifle

This popular English pudding recipe makes lots, but halves easily for family serving

Makes 12 servings.

16 thin slices pound cake (from a frozen 12-ounce pound cake)
½ cup apricot jam
1 teaspoon sherry extract
1 teaspoon rum extract
1 cup orange juice
4 cups (2 pints) strawberries, washed, hulled, and sliced
4 eggs
¼ cup granulated sugar
2 cups milk
2 teaspoons vanilla
2 cups cream for whipping
¼ cup 10X (confectioners' powdered) sugar
12 crisp macaroon cookies (from a 10-ounce package)

1 Spread 8 slices of the pound cake with apricot jam; put together, sandwich style, with remaining 8 slices, cut each crosswise into 3 strips. Arrange around side and bottom of a large shallow glass bowl.
2 Stir sherry and rum extracts into orange juice in a 1-cup measure; drizzle over cake.
3 Save about ½ cup of sliced strawberries for garnish in Step 6, then spoon remaining over cake; cover; chill.
4 Beat eggs slightly with granulated sugar and milk in top of a small double boiler. Cook, stirring constantly, over simmering, not boiling, water, 15 minutes, or until custard thickens slightly and coats a metal spoon. Strain into a medium-size bowl; stir in 1 teaspoon of the vanilla; cover; chill.
5 When ready to put dessert together, beat cream with 10X sugar and remaining 1 teaspoon vanilla until stiff in a medium-size bowl.
6 Pour chilled custard over cake and berries; stand macaroons around edge of bowl. Spoon whipped cream in mounds over custard. Pile saved strawberries in center and sprinkle with toasted slivered almonds, if you wish.
Note—Trifle can be made up several hours ahead and kept chilled until serving time. For fruit variety, try it also with canned sliced peaches or pears or pitted halved apricots.

You don't have to be English to recognize this stunning beauty, **Party Trifle.**

Chocolate Pudding

Really a custard, rich in eggs

Bake at 325° for 40 minutes.
Makes 8 servings.

    3 cups milk
    2 squares unsweetened chocolate
    4 eggs
    ⅔ cup sugar
    ¼ teaspoon salt

1 Place milk and chocolate in the top of a large double boiler. Heat over simmering water 15 minutes, or until chocolate melts and mixture is scalding; remove from heat.
2 Beat eggs slightly in a medium-size bowl; stir in sugar and salt; slowly stir in scalded milk mixture. Strain into a 6-cup baking dish.
3 Set dish in a large pan; place on oven shelf; pour boiling water into pan to within 1 inch of top of dish.
4 Bake in slow oven (325°) 40 minutes, or until center is almost set but still soft. (Do not overbake; custard will set as it cools.) Remove from water; cool; chill.
5 Spoon into dessert dishes; serve plain or top with whipped cream, if you wish.

Coffee Praline Pudding

Bread pudding really goes highfalutin here with a broiled butterscotch-nut topping over an almost-custardlike cream

Bake at 350° for 1 hour,
then broil 2 to 3 minutes.
Makes 6 servings.

    3 cups milk
    ½ cup granulated sugar
    4 teaspoons instant coffee powder
    5 tablespoons butter or margarine
    6 slices slightly dry white bread, cut in ¼-inch
        cubes
    3 eggs
    ½ teaspoon ground cinnamon
    ¼ teaspoon salt
    1 teaspoon vanilla
    ½ cup firmly packed brown sugar
    1 tablespoon cream for whipping
    ½ cup chopped walnuts

1 Heat milk with granulated sugar, instant coffee, and 3 tablespoons of the butter or marga-rine just until butter melts in a medium-size saucepan. Pour over bread cubes in a buttered 6-cup baking dish; let stand 10 minutes, then beat with a fork to blend. (Set remaining butter or margarine aside for topping in Step 4.)
2 Beat eggs slightly with cinnamon, salt, and vanilla in a small bowl; pour over bread mixture and blend in completely.
3 Bake in moderate oven (350°) 1 hour, or until a knife inserted in center comes out clean; remove from oven; turn heat to broil.
4 While pudding bakes, melt remaining 2 table-spoons butter or margarine in a small frying pan; stir in brown sugar, cream, and walnuts. Drop by small spoonfuls on top of hot pudding.
5 Broil, 4 to 6 inches from heat, 2 to 3 minutes, or just until topping bubbles up. Serve warm or cold, plain or with cream.

Molded Apricot Crown

It steams in a mold, comes out light as cake to slice and top with apricot sauce

Makes 8 servings.

    2 cans (about 1 pound each) apricot halves
    2¼ cups sifted all-purpose flour
    3 teaspoons baking powder
    1 teaspoon salt
    1 teaspoon ground cardamom
    ¼ cup (1 stick) butter or margarine
    1 cup sugar
    2 eggs
    ¾ cup milk
    ½ teaspoon lemon extract
        APRICOT SAUCE (recipe follows)

1 Grease an 8-cup tube mold well; sprinkle with sugar; tap out any excess.
2 Drain apricots; set aside 6 perfect halves for topping in Step 8; cut up enough to make ½ cup for Step 5. Save rest of fruit and syrup for sauce.
3 Measure flour, baking powder, salt, and car-damom into sifter.
4 Cream butter or margarine with sugar until fluffy in large bowl; beat in eggs.
5 Sift in dry ingredients, a third at a time, alter-nately with milk, stirring until well blended. Stir in lemon extract and ½ cup cut-up apricots.
6 Pour into prepared mold; cover with lid or foil, tying foil on tightly with string. Place on rack in large kettle or steamer; pour in boiling water to half the depth of batter in mold; cover.
7 Steam pudding 2 hours, or until a long thin metal skewer inserted near center comes out

Steamed puddings are fun, especially when topped with apricot halves, as is **Molded Apricot Crown.**

clean. (Keep water bubbling during cooking, adding more boiling water, if needed.) Cool in mold on wire rack 5 minutes.

8 Loosen around edge with knife; invert onto serving plate. Arrange 6 saved apricot halves on top; spoon ½ cup hot APRICOT SAUCE over. Cut in wedges to serve with remaining sauce.

APRICOT SAUCE

Beat saved apricot halves and syrup until smooth in blender. (Or press through a coarse sieve.) Pour into medium-size saucepan. Stir in ½ cup honey, ¼ cup (½ stick) butter or margarine, and a dash of salt. Heat to boiling; cook, uncovered, stirring often, 20 minutes, or until thick. Serve warm. Makes about 3 cups.

Fluffy Lemon Tapioca Pudding

Delicate and delicious!

Makes 6 servings.

      1 egg
  2¾ cups milk
      3 tablespoons quick-cooking tapioca
    ⅛ teaspoon salt
    ½ teaspoon vanilla
         Grated rind of ½ lemon
      3 tablespoons sugar

1 Beat egg with milk in medium-size saucepan; stir in tapioca and salt. Let stand about 5 minutes.
2 Cook, stirring constantly, 5 to 8 minutes, or until mixture comes to a full rolling boil. Remove from heat.
3 Stir in vanilla, lemon rind, and sugar; cool.
4 Spoon into 6 sherbet glasses, dividing evenly. Serve warm or chilled.

Apple Pudding Cake

Grated apples layered with buttery almond crumbs make this sweet treat to serve with whipped cream

Bake at 375° for 45 minutes.
Makes 6 to 8 servings.

6 medium-size apples
1 cup sugar
2 cups zwieback crumbs (6-ounce package)
½ cup whole blanched almonds, ground (from a 5-ounce can)
½ cup (1 stick) butter or margarine, melted

1 Pare apples, then halve, core, and grate. (There should be 4 cups.) Toss with ½ cup of the sugar in a medium-size bowl.
2 Mix zwieback crumbs, remaining ½ cup sugar, and almonds in a second medium-size bowl; blend in melted butter or margarine.
3 Layer apple and crumb mixtures into a buttered 6-cup baking dish, starting and ending with apple mixture.
4 Bake in moderate oven (375°) 45 minutes, or until apples are soft. Serve warm, plain or with whipped cream.

Christmas Pudding

Make this fruit-nut-rich classic a day ahead, if you wish. Recipe tells how to reheat

Makes 12 servings.

2½ cups sifted all-purpose flour
3 teaspoons baking powder
1 teaspoon pumpkin-pie spice
½ teaspon salt
½ cup vegetable shortening
¾ cup firmly packed brown sugar
2 eggs
1 teaspoon vanilla
¾ cup milk
½ cup (4-ounce jar) chopped mixed candied fruits
½ cup chopped walnuts
ORANGE CRYSTAL SAUCE (recipe follows)

1 Measure flour, baking powder, pumpkin-pie spice, and salt into sifter.
2 Cream shortening with brown sugar until fluffy in a large bowl; beat in eggs and vanilla.
3 Sift in dry ingredients, adding alternately with milk; beat well after each addition. Fold in candied fruits and walnuts.

4 Pour into a well-greased 8-cup mold; cover with foil, transparent wrap, or a double thickness of wax paper; fasten with string to hold tightly.
5 Place on rack or trivet in a kettle or steamer; pour in boiling water to half the depth of pudding mold; cover tightly.
6 Steam 2½ hours, or until a long thin metal skewer inserted in center comes out clean. (Keep water boiling gently during entire cooking time, adding more boiling water, if needed.)
7 Cool mold 5 minutes; loosen pudding around edge with knife; unmold onto serving plate. Spoon about ½ cup ORANGE CRYSTAL SAUCE over. Garnish with a bouquet of holly and a green and red candied cherry and walnut half, threaded onto a wooden pick, kebab style, if you wish. Cut pudding in wedges; serve with additional sauce. (To reheat pudding, wrap in foil; heat in slow oven [325°] 15 to 20 minutes, or until heated through.)

ORANGE CRYSTAL SAUCE
Combine 1 cup firmly packed light brown sugar and ½ cup orange juice in a medium-size saucepan. Heat to boiling, stirring until sugar dissolves, then simmer 5 minutes. Stir in 1 cup light corn syrup, 2 tablespoons butter or margarine, 1 tablespoon lemon juice, and ¼ teaspoon

Date-Nut Pudding

It bakes in two layers—a yummy spice sauce on the bottom and a cookie-like crust on top

Bake at 350° for 45 minutes.
Makes 6 servings.

½ cup granulated sugar
3 tablespoons butter or margarine
1½ cups sifted all-purpose flour
1½ teaspoons baking powder
½ teaspoon ground cinnamon
⅛ teaspoon salt
¾ cup milk
1 cup pitted chopped dates
½ cup chopped walnuts
½ teaspoon vanilla
½ teaspoon grated orange rind
2 cups boiling water
1 cup firmly packed brown sugar

1 Mix granulated sugar and 1 tablespoon butter or margarine in medium-size bowl.
2 Sift flour, baking powder, cinnamon, and salt onto wax paper; blend into sugar mixture alternately with milk. Stir in dates, walnuts, vanilla, and orange rind; pour into buttered pan, 9x9x2.

Combine water, brown sugar, and remaining 2 tablespoons butter or margarine in small saucepan; heat to boiling; pour over batter.

3 Bake in moderate oven (350°) 45 minutes, or until top is sticky-firm. Serve warm, with ice cream, if desired.

Pumpkin-Spice Pudding

For a snowy holiday touch, crown this rich dessert with balls of ice cream rolled in coconut

Makes 8 servings.

1½ cups sifted all-purpose flour
½ cup instant mashed-potato powder
1 teaspoon baking soda
1 teaspoon salt
1½ teaspoons pumpkin-pie spice
¼ cup (½ stick) butter or margarine
¾ cup firmly packed brown sugar
2 eggs
1 teaspoon vanilla
1 teaspoon grated orange rind
¾ cup orange juice
1 cup pumpkin (from a 1-pound can)
½ cup chopped walnuts
BUTTERSCOTCH VELVET SAUCE (recipe follows)

1 Measure flour, instant mashed-potato powder, soda, salt, and pumpkin-pie spice into a sifter.
2 Cream butter or margarine with brown sugar until fluffy in a large bowl; beat in eggs, then vanilla and orange rind.
3 Sift in dry ingredients, adding alternately with orange juice, beating well after each addition; fold in pumpkin and walnuts.
4 Pour into a well-greased 8-cup tube mold; cover with foil, transparent wrap, or double thickness of wax paper; fasten with string to hold tightly.
5 Place on a rack or trivet in a kettle or steamer; pour in boiling water to half the depth of pudding in mold; cover tightly.
6 Steam 2 hours, or until a long thin skewer inserted near center comes out clean. (Keep water boiling gently during entire time, adding more boiling water, if needed.)
7 Cool mold 5 minutes; loosen pudding around edge with a knife; unmold onto a serving plate; cool slightly. Spoon about ¼ cup hot BUTTERSCOTCH VELVET SAUCE over pudding; top with several coconut ice-cream balls, if you wish. Cut in wedges; serve with remaining sauce and additional ice-cream balls.

BUTTERSCOTCH VELVET SAUCE
Combine 1¼ cups firmly packed light brown sugar, ¼ cup cream for whipping, 2 tablespoons light corn syrup, and ¼ cup (½ stick) butter or margarine in a small saucepan. Heat to boiling, then cook 1 minute. Remove from heat; stir in 1 teaspoon vanilla. Serve hot. Makes 1¼ cups.

Chocolate Floating Islands

Meringues float like islands in a chocolate sauce

Makes 8 servings.

4 cups milk
6 eggs, separated
2 cups sugar
⅔ cup dry cocoa (not a mix)
2 teaspoons rum extract
½ teaspoon ground nutmeg
GOLDEN SUGAR RIBBONS (recipe follows)

1 Heat milk just to simmering over low heat in a large skillet with a cover.
2 Beat egg whites until foamy-white and double in volume in a large bowl. Beat in 1⅓ cups of the sugar, 1 tablespoon at a time, until meringue stands in firm peaks when the beater is lifted.
3 Scoop meringue into egg-shaped puffs with an ice cream scoop or a large spoon, making 4 at a time. Float first 4 puffs, not touching, on simmering milk, cover. Simmer over *very low* heat 5 minutes.
4 Lift meringue puffs from milk with a slotted spoon; drain on a cookie sheet covered with paper toweling; chill. Repeat, making last 4 puffs with remaining meringue; remove skillet from heat.
5 To make custard sauce: Beat egg yolks until thick in a large bowl; gradually add remaining ⅔ cup sugar. Beat in cocoa and nutmeg until well blended. Strain milk from skillet into egg yolk mixture, beating until well blended.
6 Return cocoa mixture to skillet; cook, stirring constantly, over low heat, until custard thickens slightly and coats spoon. Immediately pour into a bowl. Stir in rum extract; chill.
7 An hour before serving, pour custard sauce into a large shallow glass bowl. Float meringues gently on top; drizzle with GOLDEN SUGAR RIBBONS. Chill until ready to serve.

GOLDEN SUGAR RIBBONS
Spread ½ cup sugar in a small heavy skillet; heat slowly until sugar melts and starts to turn pale golden in color. Use immediately.

Make every dessert extra-special with a sauce that people will remember. **Jiffy Chocolate Sauce** and a melba sauce with cherries are two nobody will forget.

Sauces and Toppings

A golden glaze over a sponge pudding or a drizzle on top of ice cream. All are sauces or toppings, and you'll chance upon many favorites and new ones that you'll use over and over again.

Jiffy Chocolate Sauce

Rich and dark

Makes 1½ cups.

½ cup light cream or table cream
¼ cup water
1 cup (6-ounce package) semisweet-chocolate pieces

1 Heat cream and water just to boiling in a small saucepan; pour over semisweet-chocolate pieces in an electric-blender container; cover.
2 Beat at high speed 1 minute, or until smooth. Serve warm.

Butterscotch Sauce

Delicious on real vanilla ice cream, topped with toasted almonds

Makes 2½ cups.

2 cups firmly packed brown sugar
⅔ cup light corn syrup
¼ cup (½ stick) butter or margarine
½ cup evaporated milk
¼ cup water
1 teaspoon vanilla

1 Combine brown sugar, corn syrup, and butter or margarine in medium-size heavy saucepan; heat over low heat, stirring constantly, until butter melts and mixture is well blended.
2 Heat to boiling; cook to 230° on candy thermometer. (A little syrup will spin fine threads when dropped from tip of spoon.)
3 Remove from heat; stir in evaporated milk, water, and vanilla. Serve warm or cold.
Note—This sauce keeps well in a covered jar in the refrigerator. To reheat, place the jar, covered loosely, in a saucepan of water. Heat slowly until sauce is warm.

Fudge Sauce

Rich, dark, and thick—and a good keep-on-hand for ice cream

Makes about 1 cup.

1 cup instant cocoa mix
½ cup cream for whipping
3 tablespoons light corn syrup

1 Blend cocoa mix with cream and corn syrup in a medium-size saucepan; heat slowly, stirring constantly, just to boiling; remove from heat and let cool.
2 Serve warm or cold over ice cream, plain cake squares, or pudding or custard. (Store any leftover sauce in a tightly covered jar in the refrigerator.)

Orange Cream

For a delightful touch of citrus flavor, serve this

Makes about 2 cups.

2 egg yolks
½ cup sugar
1 tablespoon all-purpose flour
¼ teaspoon salt
¼ cup orange juice
½ teaspoon grated lemon rind
¼ cup (½ stick) butter or margarine, softened
½ cup cream for whipping

1 Beat egg yolks with sugar in top of a double boiler until thick and lemon-colored. Stir in flour and salt, then orange juice and lemon rind.
2 Cook over simmering water, adding butter or margarine about 1 tablespoon at a time and stirring constantly, 10 minutes, or until butter is melted and sauce is thick. Remove from heat; cover; chill.
3 When ready to serve, beat cream until stiff in a small bowl; fold into chilled orange mixture until no streaks of white remain.

Quick Custard Sauce

Couldn't be simpler to make with pudding
mix as your helper

Makes 4 cups.

*1 package (about 4 ounces) vanilla-flavor
  pudding mix
4 cups milk
2 tablespoons sugar
1 tablespoon butter or margarine
½ teaspoon vanilla*

1 Combine all ingredients in a medium-size
saucepan; cook, following label directions for
pudding. Remove from heat.
2 Pour into a medium-size bowl; cover. Serve
warm or chilled.

French Chocolate Fudge Sauce

Coffee cuts the sweetness in this French-
inspired sauce

Makes 1¼ cups.

*½ cup firmly packed brown sugar
1 tablespoon instant coffee powder
½ cup water
2 tablespoons light corn syrup
2 tablespoons butter or margarine
1 cup (6-ounce package) semisweet-chocolate
  pieces
1 teaspoon vanilla*

1 Combine brown sugar, instant coffee, water,
corn syrup, and butter or margarine in a small
saucepan. Heat slowly, stirring constantly, to
boiling, then cook, still stirring, 3 minutes; remove from heat.
2 Stir in semisweet-chocolate pieces and vanilla
until chocolate melts and sauce is smooth.
Serve warm. To reheat: Place in top of double
boiler over simmering water.

Toffee-Walnut Sauce

A classic combination

Makes 2 cups.

*¾ cup firmly packed light brown sugar
1 tablespoon instant coffee powder
  Dash of salt
½ cup water*

*1 can (about 14 ounces) sweetened con-
  densed milk (not evaporated)
½ cup chopped walnuts
1 teaspoon vanilla*

1 Combine brown sugar, instant coffee, salt,
and water in a small heavy saucepan; heat,
stirring constantly, to boiling, then cook, without
stirring, to 230° on a candy thermometer. (A
little syrup will spin fine threads when dropped
from tip of spoon.) Remove from heat.
2 Blend hot syrup very slowly into sweetened
condensed milk in a medium-size bowl; stir in
walnuts and vanilla. Serve warm or cold.

Mocha Sauce

Serve over pound cake squares topped with
coffee and vanilla ice creams

Makes about 2 cups.

*1 package (6 ounces) semisweet-chocolate
  pieces (1 cup)
¼ cup (½ stick) butter or margarine
1 cup sifted 10X (confectioners' powdered)
  sugar
½ cup light corn syrup
2 teaspoons instant coffee powder
  Dash of salt
½ cup hot water
1 teaspoon vanilla*

1 Melt chocolate pieces with butter or margarine in top of a double boiler over simmering
water.
2 Stir in sugar, corn syrup, instant coffee, salt,
hot water and vanilla until sauce is smooth and
slightly thickened. Remove from heat. Serve at
room temperature.

Golden Butterscotch Sauce

A translucent version of the traditional recipe

Makes about 1½ cups.

*2 cups firmly packed brown sugar
¼ cup dark corn syrup
3 tablespoons water
1 tablespoon lemon juice
¾ teaspoon salt
1 tablespoon butter or margarine
1 teaspoon vanilla*

1 Mix sugar, corn syrup, water, lemon juice and salt in medium-size saucepan; heat slowly, stirring until sugar is dissolved; add butter or margarine.

2 Heat to boiling; cook, without stirring, until candy thermometer reads 230° (or until a fine thread spins from the end of a fork when dipped into hot syrup).

3 Remove from heat; stir in vanilla; cool.

Mock Zabaglione

An extra-rich soft custard sauce for fresh or canned fruits, fruit whips, or gelatin desserts

Makes 1¼ cups.

4 egg yolks
4 tablespoons 10X (confectioners' powdered) sugar
1 cup half-and-half (milk and cream)
1 teaspoon sherry or rum flavoring
½ teaspoon vanilla

1 Beat egg yolks until creamy-thick in top of a double boiler; beat in 10X sugar gradually; stir in half-and-half.

2 Cook, stirring constantly, over simmering, *not boiling,* water until sauce thickens slightly and coats a metal spoon; remove from heat; strain into a small bowl.

3 Stir in sherry or rum flavoring and vanilla. Serve warm or chilled.

Ice-Cream Sauce

It tastes like softened vanilla ice cream, looks like whipped cream. Scrumptious on deep-dish pie or pudding

Makes about 2¼ cups.

1 egg
3 tablespoons sugar
Dash of salt
¼ cup (½ stick) butter or margarine, melted
½ teaspoon vanilla
¾ cup cream for whipping

1 Beat egg with sugar and salt until fluffy-thick in a medium-size bowl; beat in melted butter or margarine, a small amount at a time; stir in vanilla.

2 Beat cream until stiff in a small bowl; fold into egg-sugar mixture until no streaks of white remain.

Regal Burnt-Sugar Sauce

Rightly named, for it's delectably sweet and clear as crystal. Drizzle over ice cream or baked custard

Makes about 2 cups.

1½ cups sugar
1 cup boiling water

1 Heat sugar in a medium-size heavy frying pan over low heat, stirring constantly with a wooden spoon, until melted into a golden syrup; remove from heat.

2 Stir in water *very slowly.* (Watch it, for mixture will spatter.) Return to heat; cook, stirring constantly, until smooth and syrupy. (Sauce will be thin, but will thicken as it cools.) Serve warm or cold.

Sauce Brasilia

Freshly brewed coffee is the main ingredient. Spoon over angel or spongecake wedges or chocolate soufflé

Makes 2 cups.

¾ cup sugar
2 tablespoons cornstarch
Dash of salt
1½ cups freshly brewed strong coffee
2 tablespoons butter or margarine
2 teaspoons vanilla

1 Combine sugar, cornstarch, and salt in a medium-size saucepan; stir in coffee until mixture is smooth.

2 Cook, stirring constantly, over medium heat, until sauce thickens and boils 3 minutes; remove from heat.

3 Stir in butter or margarine until melted, and vanilla. Serve warm.

Mock Crème de Menthe

Perfect with pineapple sherbet or canned or fresh pineapple chunks

Makes ½ cup.

½ cup light corn syrup
1½ teaspoons peppermint extract
Few drops green food coloring

(continued)

Combine corn syrup and peppermint extract in a 1-cup measure; stir in green food coloring to tint a bright green.

Pudding-Best Pudding Sauce

Whip it up with instant pudding mix; serve on steamed or baked puddings

Makes 4 cups.

1 package (about 4 ounces) vanilla-or chocolate-flavor instant pudding mix
¼ cup 10X (confectioners' powdered) sugar
3 cups milk
1 teaspoon vanilla
½ cup cream for whipping

1 Combine pudding mix, 10X sugar, milk, and vanilla in a medium-size bowl; beat 1 minute with rotary or electric beater.
2 Beat cream until stiff in a small bowl; fold into pudding mixture; cover. Chill at least 1 hour.

Tart Melba Sauce

Traditionally served with peaches and ice cream, but equally luscious on vanilla or tapioca puddings

Makes about 1 cup.

1 package (10 ounces) frozen red raspberries,
 thawed
⅔ cup sugar
 Pinch of cream of tartar

1 Press thawed raspberries through a sieve into a small saucepan; discard seeds. Stir in sugar and cream of tartar.
2 Heat quickly, stirring constantly, to boiling, then cook, still stirring, 3 minutes, or until slightly thick. Pour into a small bowl; cover; chill.

Strawberry Hard Sauce

Flavored, or plain, this sauce is a classic for steamed puddings

Makes about 1 cup.

¼ cup (½ stick) margarine
1½ cups 10X (confectioners' powdered) sugar
 2 tablespoons crushed fresh strawberries

1 Cream margarine until fluffy in a small bowl. (Be sure to use margarine, *not butter,* so mixture will not separate.)
2 Beat in 10X sugar, a little at a time, until blended, then beat in strawberries until smooth; cover; chill.

 PLAIN HARD SAUCE: Use butter or margarine and substitute 1 teaspoon vanilla or rum flavoring for the strawberries. Sprinkle with freshly grated nutmeg before serving.

Golden Fruit Sauce

Versatile fruit cocktail makes this sparkler for plain cake squares, custard, rice or other puddings

Makes about 2 cups.

1 can (about 1 pound) fruit cocktail
1 tablespoon cornstarch
2 tablespoons lemon juice
1½ teaspoons grated lemon rind

1 Drain syrup from fruit cocktail into a cup. Set fruit aside for Step 3.
2 Blend cornstarch into a few tablespoons of the syrup until smooth in a small saucepan, then stir in remaining syrup and lemon juice.
3 Cook, stirring constantly, over medium heat, until sauce thickens and boils 3 minutes; stir in fruit and lemon rind. Serve warm.

Hilo Fruit Sauce

Your choice of fruits "poach" in this sauce

Makes about ¾ cup.

¾ cup pineapple juice
¾ cup firmly packed brown sugar
 2 tablespoons lemon juice
½ teaspoon ground ginger

1 Combine all ingredients in a medium-size frying pan or chafing dish; heat to boiling, then simmer 10 minutes to thicken slightly and blend flavors.
2 Lay fresh or canned fruits, cut in serving-size pieces, in syrup. Heat, basting with syrup, just until heated through, then sprinkle with coconut. Serve warm.

Creamy Rum Sauce

A lighter alternative to hard sauce

Makes 3 cups.

1 egg
¼ cup sugar
 Dash of salt
¼ cup (½ stick) butter or margarine
½ teaspoon rum flavoring extract
1 cup cream for whipping

1 Heat egg in the top of a small double boiler over simmering water, beating all the time and adding sugar gradually until mixture is creamy-thick; stir in salt. (Beating will take about two minutes.)
2 Beat in butter or margarine, a thin slice at a time, keeping top over simmering water and beating constantly, until creamy again. Pour into a bowl; stir in rum flavoring; Chill until ready to serve.
3 Beat cream until stiff in a medium-size bowl; spoon on top of chilled mixture and fold in. (Tip: Use a portable electric mixer for beating and plan to use the sauce up the first time around—it tends to lose its fluffiness upon standing.)

VARIATIONS:

Fluffy Vanilla Sauce: *Prepare as directed for* CREAMY RUM SAUCE *but substitute 1 teaspoon vanilla for the rum flavoring extract.*
Fluffy Wine Sauce: *Prepare as directed for* CREAMY RUM SAUCE *but substitute 1 tablespoon cream sherry, ruby port or sweet Madeira wine for the rum flavoring extract.*

Maple Fluff Sauce

A simple Vermont idea

Makes about 1½ cups.

1 cup blended maple syrup
1 cup tiny marshmallows

Place all ingredients in the top of a double boiler, set over simmering water and heat and stir until creamy-smooth. Serve warm or cold. Store in refrigerator.

Marshmallow Sauce

Few things are better over homemade ice cream

Makes about 1½ cups.

½ cup light corn syrup
½ cup light cream or table cream
1 cup tiny marshmallows
½ teaspoon vanilla

Place corn syrup, cream and marshmallows in the top of a double boiler, set over simmering water and heat and stir until creamy-smooth. Remove from heat, stir in vanilla. Serve warm or cold. Store in refrigerator.

Coconut-Lemon Sauce

Nippy lemon and nutmeg blend invitingly

Makes 1¾ cups.

½ cup sugar
5 teaspoons cornstarch
⅛ teaspoon salt
⅛ teaspoon nutmeg
1 cup water
2 tablespoons lemon juice
¼ cup flaked coconut (from a 3½-ounce can)
2 teaspoons grated lemon rind
2 tablespoons butter or margarine

1 Mix sugar, cornstarch, salt, and nutmeg in a small saucepan; stir in water and lemon juice until mixture is smooth. Cook, stirring constantly, over medium heat until sauce thickens and boils 3 minutes; remove from heat.
2 Stir in coconut, lemon rind, and butter or margarine until butter melts. Serve warm.

Pink Peppermint Sauce

Very bracing

Makes about 1¼ cups.

1 cup bottled marshmallow topping
¼ cup light corn syrup
½ cup crushed pink peppermint candies
 Few drops red food coloring

Place all ingredients in the top of a double boiler, set over simmering water and heat and stir until creamy-smooth. Serve warm or cold. Store in refrigerator.

Hot Fudge Sauce

Hot sauce goes so well with cold ice cream

Makes about 1 cup.

¾ cup light corn syrup
½ cup dry cocoa (not a mix)
  Dash of salt
⅓ cup butter or margarine
½ teaspoon vanilla

1 Combine syrup, cocoa and salt in a small saucepan. Heat slowly, stirring constantly, to boiling; simmer 3 minutes. Remove from heat.
2 Stir in butter or margarine and vanilla. Serve warm over ice cream or vanilla pudding.

Fast Fudge Sauce

Make this ahead of time

Makes about 1 cup.

1 cup semisweet-chocolate pieces
¾ cup light corn syrup
¼ cup milk
1 tablespoon butter or margarine
½ teaspoon vanilla

Place all ingredients in the top of a double boiler, set over simmering water and heat until smooth and creamy. Store in refrigerator.

Toffee-Almond Sauce

Drizzle this super-rich creamy sauce over ice cream or squares of plain cake topped with whipped cream

Makes 2 cups.

¾ cup firmly packed light brown sugar
1 tablespoon instant coffee powder
  Dash of salt
½ cup water
1 can (about 14 ounces) sweetened condensed milk
½ cup chopped toasted almonds
1 teaspoon almond extract

1 Combine brown sugar, instant coffee, salt and water in a small heavy saucepan; heat, stirring constantly, to boiling, then cook, without stirring, to 230° on a candy thermometer. (A little syrup will spin fine threads when dropped from tip of spoon.) Remove from heat.
2 Blend hot syrup very slowly into sweetened condensed (not evaporated) milk in a medium-size bowl; stir in almonds and extract. Serve warm or cold.

Praline Sauce

Like liquid candy!

Makes 1½ cups.

1 cup firmly packed dark brown sugar
½ cup light corn syrup
¼ cup (½ stick) butter or margarine
⅛ teaspoon salt
½ cup chopped pecans

1 Combine sugar, corn syrup, butter or margarine and salt in a medium-size saucepan. Cook over low heat, stirring constantly, until sugar dissolves. Bring to boiling; boil 2 minutes.
2 Remove from heat and mix in pecans. Serve warm.

Mint Fudge Sauce

Serve over mint chocolate chip ice cream

Makes 1¼ cups.

1 package (about 8¼ ounces) mint-flavor chocolate candy wafers
½ cup evaporated milk

Heat candy wafers and evaporated milk in the top of a double boiler, set over simmering water, stirring often, just until candy is melted and smooth. Serve warm or cold. Store in refrigerator.

Chocolate Truffle Sauce

So velvety and rich!

Makes about 1 cup.

1 package (6 ounces) semisweet-chocolate pieces
¾ cup eggnog (from a 4-cup container)

Melt semisweet-chocolate pieces in top of a

double boiler over simmering water. Stir in egg-nog until well blended. Serve warm or cold. Store in refrigerator.

Chocolate Velvet Sauce

The texture's smooth, the taste—gorgeous

Makes 1 cup.

½ pound (32) marshmallows
2 squares (1 ounce each) unsweetened choc-
    olate
½ cup evaporated milk
1 teaspoon vanilla

Melt marshmallows and chocolate in the top of a double boiler over simmering water, stirring often, until creamy-smooth. Gradually blend in evaporated milk; stir in vanilla. Serve warm or cold. Store in refrigerator.

Brandy Butterscotch Sauce

Yet another version

Makes 1 cup.

1¼ cups firmly packed light brown sugar
½ cup light cream or table cream
2 tablespoons light corn syrup
4 tablespoons butter or margarine
1 teaspoon brandy extract

Combine brown sugar, cream, corn syrup and butter or margarine in a small saucepan. Heat to boiling; boil 1 minute. Remove from heat and stir in brandy extract. Serve warm or cold. Store in refrigerator.

Caramel-Walnut Sauce

Try this over apple dumplings

Makes about 1½ cups.

½ pound caramel-candy cubes
¾ cup water
½ cup chopped walnuts

Place caramels and water in the top of a double

boiler, set over simmering water and heat and stir until smooth and creamy. Mix in nuts. Store in refrigerator.

Chocolate Sundae Sauce

A good basic sauce

Makes 1 cup.

1 package (6 ounces) semisweet-chocolate
    pieces
2 tablespoons butter or margarine
1 cup sifted 10X (confectioners' powdered)
    sugar
½ cup hot milk
1 teaspoon vanilla

1 Combine semisweet-chocolate pieces and butter or margarine in top of small double boiler; heat over simmering water, stirring often, 10 to 12 minutes, or until chocolate is melted.
2 Add 10X sugar alternately with hot milk; beat until smooth; stir in vanilla; serve warm or cold over your favorite ice cream.

Chocolate-Nut Sauce

Makes about 1¼ cups.

¼ cup (½ stick) butter or margarine
2 tablespoons light corn syrup
1 cup (6-ounce package) semisweet-chocolate
    pieces
1 cup chopped walnuts

Melt butter or margarine in small heavy sauce-pan; remove from heat. Blend in corn syrup; stir in semisweet-chocolate pieces until almost melted, then walnuts. Serve warm.

Easy Mocha Sauce

Whip this up for a last minute dessert without last minute haste

Makes 1¼ cups.

1 package chocolate-flavor instant-pudding
    mix
1 tablespoon instant coffee powder
1 cup light corn syrup
¼ cup warm water

(continued)

Blend instant-pudding mix, instant coffee powder and corn syrup in a small bowl; stir in ¼ cup water just until smooth. Store in refrigerator.

Java Sauce

Coffee lovers can never get enough!

Makes about 1½ cups.

2 tablespoons instant coffee powder
½ cup cream for whipping
1 cup light corn syrup

Place all ingredients in the top of a double boiler, set over simmering water and heat and stir until creamy-smooth. Serve warm or cold. Store in refrigerator.

Orange-Butterscotch Sauce

Great with sherbet

Makes about 1½ cups.

2 cups firmly packed brown sugar
¼ cup dark corn syrup
3 tablespoons water
1 tablespoon orange juice
¾ teaspoon salt
1 tablespoon butter or margarine
1 teaspoon orange extract

1 Mix sugar, corn syrup, water, orange juice and salt in medium-size saucepan; heat slowly, stirring until sugar is dissolved; add butter or margarine.
2 Heat to boiling; cook, without stirring, until candy thermometer reads 230° (or until a fine thread spins from the end of a fork when dipped into hot syrup).
3 Remove from heat; stir in orange extract; cool.

Sparkle Ice-Cream Sauce

It goes together with no fussy syrup cooking and keeps its sparkle to the last drop

Makes 4 cups.

2 cups firmly packed light brown sugar
1 cup water

2 cups (1-pint bottle) light corn syrup
½ teaspoon salt

Combine brown sugar and water in a medium-size saucepan. Heat to boiling, stirring until brown sugar dissolves, then cook 5 minutes; remove from heat. Stir in corn syrup and salt; cool.

WHIPPED TOPPINGS

Low-calorie whipped-topping mix— Weight-watchers can enjoy heaps of this snowy wonder for just about seven calories per tablespoonful. While the package costs more than regular whipped-topping mixes, it makes about twice as much. Note that label directions, to hold the calorie line, call for water in place of milk.

Toppings in pressurized cans—These press-and-serve specialties are stocked by some supermarkets in the dairy case; by others, in frozen-food cabinets next to ice creams or fruits. Remember that there are two kinds—dairy and nondairy—and be sure you know how they differ. The dairy type blends milk solids, sugar, and flavoring with actual cream; the nondairy version has a base of liquid vegetable oil and contains no cream, milk, or milk fat.
  At home, store these products in the refrigerator or freezer, according to label directions. Though tops in convenience and airy light, they do not hold up well, so add them to foods just before serving.
Frozen toppings—Ready-whipped non- dairy topping is the newest of all. It comes in plastic containers to spoon—still frozen, or thawed first, as you prefer—over fruit, shortcake, pudding, virtually any dessert. Besides being handily ready to use, it has another big advantage: You can take out what you need for one meal and keep the rest in freezer or refrigerator for another time. In some regions, you'll also find half-pint containers of a frozen nondairy topper that you whip yourself.
Instant nonfat dry milk and evaporated milk—These dependables pamper your family and your budget at the same time. Simply combine the dry milk powder with ice water, and it will whip to a billowy cloud for barely 2¢ a cupful. Evaporated milk, when freezer-cold and beaten up, triples in volume, at about one third the cost and calories of whipping cream.

INDEX

A-B

Alaska
  Cantaloupe, 33
  Royal Baked, 32
  Walnut Bombe, 30
Apples
  Apple-Cinnamon Ice Cream, 37
  Apple-Mint Charlotte, 66
  Apple-Raisin Crisp, 20
  Butterscotch Apple Cake, 17
  Devonshire Pie, 16
  Dumplings with Raspberry
    Sauce, 17
  Pudding Cake, 84
  Stuffed Baked, 19
Applesauce Cobbler Cake, 21
Apricot
  Bavarian, 50
  Molded Crown, 82
  Rice-Pudding Pie, 11
Banana Split Pie, 22
Bavarian
  Apricot, 50
  Chocolate Velvet, 50
  Royale, 49
  Mocha, 50
Biscuit Tortoni, 37
Black Walnut Chess Pie, 60
Bombe
  Dublin Ice-Cream, 29
  Hazelnut Cream, 29
  Walnut Alaska, 30
Brandied Peach Ice Cream, 37
Brandy Butterscotch Sauce, 93
Bread Pudding, Cinnamon-Raisin, 70
Brownie Sundae Shortcake, 25
Bunny Sundae, 27
Burnt-Sugar Sauce, Regal, 89
Buttermilk-Lime Sherbet, 38
Butterscotch
  Apple Cake, 17
  Brandy Sauce, 93
  Golden Sauce, 88
  Orange-Butterscotch Sauce, 94
  Quick Sundae, 26
  Sauce, 87

C

Café Cream Royale, 77
Café Cream Cups, 76
Cake
  Apple Pudding, 84
  Applesauce Cobbler, 21
  Butterscotch Apple, 17
  Minted Pineapple, 7
  Pineapple Chiffon, 9
  Rainbow Ice-Cream, 32
  Spanish Wind, 41
  Sponge, 71
  Sugared Lemon Crown, 21
Calypso Sundae, 27
Cantaloupe Alaska, 33
Cantaloupe Cream Melba, 12
Caramel Cups, 71
Caramel-Walnut Sauce, 93
Carolina Melon Salad, 10
Charlotte
  Apple-Mint, 66

Maple Butter-Nut, 35
Raspberry Chiffon, 51
Cheese
  Frozen Eggnog Squares, 38
  Strawberry Mold, 55
Cheesecake
  Chocolate Ripple, 47
  Family Circle's Best, 49
  Fruit Crown, 8
  Lemon, 47
  Royal Cheddar, 48
Cherry Cordial Chocolate Soufflé, 73
Chess Pies
  Black Walnut, 60
  Chocolate Brownie, 60
  French Lemon, 60
  Raspberry-Pear, 59
  Southern, 61
  Strawberry-Nectar, 62
Chocolate
  Brownie Pie, 60
  Cherry Cordial Soufflé, 73
  Floating Islands, 84
  French Fudge Sauce, 88
  Ice Cream Supreme, 34
  Jiffy Sauce, 87
  Milk-Chocolate Mousse, 34
  Mint Parfait, 28
  Nut Sauce, 93
  Pudding, 82
  Regal Hot Soufflé, 73
  Ripple Cheesecake, 47
  Sundae Sauce, 93
  Truffle Sauce, 92
  Velvet Bavarian, 50
  Velvet Sauce, 93
Christmas Pudding, 84
Cinnamon-Raisin Bread Pudding, 70
Coconut-Lemon Sauce, 91
Coffee-Almond Sparkle Sundae, 26
Coffee Meringue Glacé, 33
Coffee Praline Pudding, 82
Compote
  Molded Grape, 19
  Shortcake, 59
Cranberry Ice, 39
Cranberry Tortoni, 37
Crème
  Brulée, 78
  Café Cream Royale, 77
  Honey-Spice Yule Logs, 77
  Mexican, 80
  Nesselrode Cream Mold, 78
Crème de Menthe, Mock, 89
Custard
  Caramel Cups, 71
  Crown, 73
  Eggs in Snow, 69
  Perfect, 71
  Pots de Crème au Chocolat, 69
  Quick Sauce, 88

D-G

Date-Nut Pudding, 84
Devonshire Apple Pie, 16
Dublin Ice-Cream Bombe, 29
Eggnog Cheese Squares, Frozen, 38
Eggs in Snow, 69

Family Circle's Best Cheesecake, 49
Flan, Triple Fruit, 19
Fluffy Lemon Tapioca Pudding, 83
French Lemon Pie, 60
Fruit Crown Cheesecake, 8
Fudge Sauce, 87
  Fast, 92
Gelatin
  Peach Melba, 54
  Rice Mold Imperial, 54
  Rosé Ring, 54
  Strawberries on-the-Half-Shell, 52
  Strawberry Cheese Mold, 55
  Strawberry Mousse, 52
Glacé
  Coffee Meringue, 33
  Orange Pouf, 65
  Strawberry Surprise, 14
Glazed Ruby Tartlets, 63
Golden Butterscotch Sauce, 88
Golden Fruit Sauce, 90
Grape Ice, 39

H-L

Hazelnut Cream Bombe, 29
Hilo Fruit Sauce, 90
Honey-Butter Sundae, 26
Honeydew Horn of Plenty, 12
Honey-Spice Yule Logs, 77
Hot Fudge Sauce, 92
Hot Fudge Sundae, 25
Ice
  Cranberry, 39
  Grape, 39
  Italian, 39
  Watermelon, 12
Ice Cream
  Apple-Cinnamon, 37
  Brandied Peach, 37
  Chocolate Supreme, 34
  Old-Fashioned Vanilla, 34
  Orange Blossom, 36
  Rainbow Cake, 32
  Italian Ice, 39
Java Sauce, 94
Kona Sundae, 26
Lemon
  Angel Torte, 42
  Blossom Tart, 22
  Cheesecake, 47
  Coconut-Lemon Sauce, 91
  Cool Cream Soufflé, 75
  Fluffy Tapioca Pudding, 83
  French Pie, 60
  Hot Soufflé, 75
  Meringue Tarts, 7
  Snow Sherbet, 39
  Sugared Crown, 21

M-R

Maple Butter-Nut Charlotte, 35
Maple Fluff Sauce, 91
Marshmallow Sauce, 91
Melba
  Cantaloupe Cream, 12
  Peach, 54
  Tart Sauce, 90

Melon
  Carolina Salad, 10
  in Sabayon Sauce, 10
Meringue
  Apple Mint Charlotte, 66
  Eggs in Snow, 69
  Orange Pouf Glacé, 65
  Peach Crown, 65
  Shells, 66
Mexican Cream Torte, 30
Mexican Crème, 80
Milk-Chocolate Mousse, 34
Mincemeat-Pear Pie, 63
Minted Pineapple Cake, 7
Mint Fudge Sauce, 92
Mocha Bavarian, 50
Mocha Sauce, 88
Mock Crème de Menthe, 89
Mock Zabaglione, 89
Molded Apricot Crown, 82
Molded Grape Compote, 19
Moore-Betty's Trifle, 70
Mousse
  Milk-Chocolate, 34
  Raspberry, 35
  Strawberry, 52
Nesselrode Cream Mold, 78
Old-Fashioned Vanilla Ice Cream, 34
Orange Blossom Ice Cream, 36
Orange-Butterscotch Sauce, 94
Orange Cream, 87
Orange Pouf Glacé, 65
Papaya Cream, Frozen, 8
Parfait
  Chocolate Mint, 28
  Paradise, 29
Party Pink Pouf, 42
Peach Fiesta Split, 27
Peach Melba, 54
Peach-Orange Sherbet, "Instant," 38
Pears
  Mincemeat-Pear Pie, 63
  Raspberry-Pear Pie, 59
  Splits, 28
Peppermint Sauce, Pink, 91
Peppermint Snowballs, 28
Pie
  Apricot Rice-Pudding, 11
  Banana Split, 22
  Devonshire Apple, 16
  Lemon Dream, 21
  Mincemeat-Pear, 63
  Rainbow Party, 33
  Raisin Cream, 64
Pineapple
  Chiffon Cake, 9
  Minted Cake, 7
  Sherbet in Orange Cups, 38
Plum Sherbet, 10
Pots de Crème au Chocolat, 69
Praline Sauce, 92
Pudding
  Apple Cake, 84
  Best Sauce, 90
  Chocolate, 82
  Chocolate Floating Island, 85
  Christmas, 84
  Cinnamon-Raisin Bread, 70
  Coffee Praline, 82
  Date-Nut, 84
  Fluffy Lemon Tapioca, 83
  Molded Apricot Crown, 82
  Party Trifle, 80
  Pumpkin-Spice, 85
  Summer Surprise, 8

Pumpkin-Spice Pudding, 85
Rainbow Ice-Cream Cake, 32
Rainbow Party Pie, 33
Raisins
  Apple-Raisin Crisp, 20
  Raisin Cream Pie, 64
Raspberry Chiffon Charlotte, 51
Raspberry Mousse, 35
Raspberry-Pear Pie, 59
Raspberry Sauce, 17
Rice Mold Imperial, 54
Rice-Pudding Pie, Apricot, 11
Rosé Ring, 54
Royal Baked Alaska, 32
Royal Cheddar Cheesecake, 48
Royal Fruit Tart, 13
Royal Hot Chocolate Soufflé, 73
Rum Sauce, Creamy, 91

S

Sauce
  Best Pudding, 90
  Brandy Butterscotch, 93
  Brasilia, 89
  Butterscotch, 87
  Caramel-Walnut, 93
  Chocolate-Nut, 93
  Chocolate Sundae, 93
  Chocolate Truffle, 92
  Chocolate Velvet, 93
  Coconut-Lemon, 91
  Creamy Rum, 91
  Easy Mocha, 93
  Fast Fudge, 92
  French Chocolate Fudge, 88
  Fudge, 87
  Golden Butterscotch, 88
  Golden Fruit, 90
  Hilo Fruit, 90
  Hot Fudge, 92
  Ice-Cream, 89
  Java, 94
  Jiffy Chocolate, 87
  Maple Fluff, 91
  Marshmallow, 91
  Mint Fudge, 92
  Mocha, 88
  Mock Crème de Menthe, 89
  Mock Zabaglione, 89
  Orange-Butterscotch, 94
  Orange Cream, 87
  Pink Peppermint, 91
  Praline, 92
  Quick Custard, 88
  Regal Burnt-Sugar, 89
  Rio Chocolate, 25
  Sabayon, 10
  Sparkle Ice-Cream, 94
  Strawberry Hard, 90
  Tart Melba, 90
  Toffee-Almond, 92
  Toffee-Walnut, 88
Sherbet
  Buttermilk-Lime, 38
  "Instant" Peach-Orange, 38
  Lemon Snow, 39
  Pineapple in Orange Cups, 38
  Plum, 10
Shortcake
  Compote, 59
  Imperial Strawberry, 57
  Strawberry-Rhubarb, 16
Sinker Sundae, 26
Soufflé
  Café Cream Cups, 76

Cherry Cordial Chocolate, 73
Cool Lemon Cream, 75
Hot Lemon, 75
Regal Hot Chocolate, 73
Southern Chess Pie, 61
Spanische Windtorte, 41
Sparkle Ice-Cream Sauce, 94
Split
  Banana Pie, 22
  Peach Fiesta, 27
  Pear, 28
Sponge Cake, 71
Strawberries
  Chantilly, 13
  Chantilly Torte, 45
  Chiffon Tarts, 14
  Frozen Crown, 31
  Glacé Surprise, 14
  on-the-Half-Shell, 52
  Hard Sauce, 90
  Imperial Shortcake, 57
  Mousse, 52
  Nectar Pie, 62
  Parisienne, 16
  Shortcake Seville, 57
  Strawberry-Rhubarb Shortcake, 16
Stuffed Baked Apples, 19
Sugared Lemon Crown, 21
Summer Pudding Surprise, 8
Sundaes
  Brownie Shortcakes, 25
  Bunny, 27
  Calypso, 27
  Coffee-Almond Sparkle, 26
  Honey-Butter, 26
  Hot Fudge, 25
  Jubilee Stacks, 27
  Kona, 26
  Quick Butterscotch, 26
  Regal Rio, 25
  Sinker, 26
Sweet Pastry Tart Shells, 53

T-Z

Tart
  Glazed Ruby Tartlets, 63
  Lemon Blossom, 22
  Lemon Meringue, 7
  Royal Fruit, 13
  Strawberry-Chiffon, 14
Tart Melba Sauce, 90
Tart Shells, Sweet Pastry, 53
Toffee-Almond Sauce, 92
Toffee-Walnut Sauce, 88
Topping, Whipped, 94
Torte
  Lemon Angel, 42
  Mexican Cream, 30
  Party Pink Pouf, 42
  Raspberry Angel, 44
  Spanische Windtorte, 41
  Strawberry Chantilly, 45
Tortoni
  Biscuit, 37
  Cranberry, 37
Trifle
  Maurice Moore-Betty's, 70
  Party, 80
Triple Fruit Flan, 19
Walnuts
  Toffee-Walnut Sauce, 88
  Bombe Alaska, 30
Watermelon Ice, 12
Whipped Topping, 94
Zabaglione, Mock, 89